# MICHAEL PALIN

## New Europe

## PHOTOGRAPHS BY BASIL PAO

T0114999

DESIGN & ART DIRECTION BY DAVID ROWLEY

WEIDENFELD & NICOLSON

# Contents

For Archie

# Introduction

MANY TIMES, too many times, I've woken, 35,000 feet in the air, in that limbo-land between the end of an old day and the start of a new one, after a long flight from somewhere far away. I've pushed up the window shutter and peered out at the twinkling lights below and wanted to be down there, in a real house with a kitchen table and eggs on the stove and coffee on the hob.

More often than not, it's eastern Europe that I see waking up below me and though it's only two hours from where I live, I realise with a jolt that I know more about Hong Kong or the Hindu Kush than what it's really like down there.

Of all the continents I've touched in the nineteen heady years since we started out on *Around the World in Eighty Days*, Europe is the one in which I've lingered least, partly because it is so close to home, and partly because much of it has been in serious disarray. Our planes were bombing Serbia only eight years ago.

But since the start of the twenty-first century Europe has begun to sort itself out. East and West have drawn closer. There have been no major conflicts. Countries once suspicious of visitors now welcome them with open arms.

So when it came to reuniting Saga Platoon for one more adventure it seemed that there was a gap to be filled. The continent I had flown over on so many dark mornings could not be ignored any longer. It was time for Europe. And time to get out my trusty, increasingly tattered, Penguin Encyclopaedia of Places.

*'Europe: Apart from Australia, the smallest of the continents. It occupies about seven per cent of the earth's land surface. On the other hand it is second to Asia for size of population, containing over 20 per cent of the world total.'*

And therein lay the first problem. An awful lot of people to meet.

It became clear that it would take us too long to cover the whole of Europe. Most interesting to me was that half of my own continent which, for most of my lifetime, was chilled by a Cold War and concealed behind an Iron Curtain. Now, with the Cold War over and the Iron Curtain lifted, there was the prospect of being able to travel through once-forbidden lands; of making a voyage of discovery on my very own doorstep.

Trying to describe such a journey in purely geographical terms didn't seem quite right. Some countries were clearly part of Eastern Europe, others very definitely Central Europe, while others, like Turkey, Moldova or Ukraine, didn't fit into either category. What they all seemed to have in common was a sense of rapid change, an opening-up of new horizons. It wasn't just names that were changing. Opportunities were being seized, old systems challenged, economic and political alliances entirely rethought. Nothing was quite as it had been before. Peoples, cultures and traditions with long historical roots were being shaken up and re-energised. Compared to the relatively secure and settled shape of Western Europe, the realignment of the eastern half of the continent was hurtling along. What was taking shape, both on the map and in the head was a new Europe. Or as we say on television, a New Europe.

If I'd made this journey eighteen years ago, instead of haring off around the world, it would have taken me through ten countries. Today there are twenty. More than all the countries in our Himalaya and Sahara journeys put together.

Many of these new nations are tiny, some with total populations smaller than that of London, but despite their size they have a very clear sense of their own identity, reinforced and defined by their own language, culture, history and currency. What makes their existence viable is the supportive hand of the European Union. Not all are part of it yet, but all feel that its benefits are worth taking seriously. After a century of power struggles which have visited unimaginable horrors upon the continent this coming-together is breathtakingly fresh and promising.

So I set out with considerable excitement in May 2006, and, a year later I find myself neither disillusioned nor cynical. The spirit of New Europe does exist, the hopes and dreams still burn and the future is full of opportunity. Our journey might just have been through a very small window in history and my natural tendency to optimism and half-full glasses may have misled me, but whatever the future holds I think it is important to have marked this moment when, for the first time in a thousand years, the old Europe of domination and conflict has been replaced by a new Europe of co-operation.

Let's, for all our sakes, hope that we can make it work.

### THE JOURNEY

We filmed over a period of twenty-two weeks between 16 May 2006 and 4 May 2007, generally avoiding the very depths of winter, though snow and ice caught up with us in Turkey. My formative impressions of Eastern Europe had been in monochrome, as if the people there lived in concrete apartment blocks under permanently grey skies. Basil Pao's pictures for the book and Nigel Meakin's photographs for the BBC series are an eloquent corrective. The sun shone throughout most of our journey. Though there are far too many concrete blocks, we also saw well-kept, elegant, ancient and very beautiful cities and villages, as well as swathes of countryside farmed by the traditional methods fast disappearing from west European landscapes.

And though the mountains may not be the Himalayas, there was snow on the tops of the Carpathians and the Julian Alps in the middle of summer.

The book is made up from my diary notes, with one exception. For the first time on any of my travels I had my shoulder bag stolen. It happened on my arrival in Budapest and though I lost phone and money neither mattered a damn compared to the loss of my little black book containing all my notes on the Baltic states. There was nothing I could do but sit in my hotel room overlooking the Danube and recreate it all from memory and from muttered observations on my voice recorder. It's a tribute to the Baltics that so much came back so vividly. If some days are missed out, it's because they were rest days.

# Postscript

Even allowing for the fact that life abroad is much worse when you read about it in the newspapers than when you're actually there, some ominous clouds are gathering on the horizons of new Europe.

Romania and Bulgaria have joined the European Union since I set out, but the likelihood of an independent Kosovo could ruffle the Balkans again. There are many who disagree with Poland's new anti-communist vetting laws (which have already tarnished the reputation of Ryszard Kapuscinski, one of their country's finest travellers and journalists). Turkey is having increasing difficulty balancing its secular tradition with Islamist aspirations, and Ukrainian politicians are still nowhere near resolving the rift between the eastern- and western-oriented halves of the country. There have been student riots in Hungary, and Russia and Estonia have come to serious blows after the relocation of a war memorial.

At least these are problems the countries of the region will have to sort out themselves. Far more worrying is that super-power politics, from whose corrosive influence Europe looked to have been mercifully released, is back on the agenda. At the time of writing the Americans and the Russians seem hell-bent on resurrecting the Cold War.

My advice would be, as you might expect, not to stay at home and worry, but to go to the countries and find out for yourselves.

MICHAEL PALIN, LONDON, JUNE 2007

A PRACTICAL MAP OF
# NEW EUROPE

---------- Denotes route taken by Mr Palin

► Denotes direction of travel

| 60 | 90 |
|----|----|

Ukraine

Moldova

Black Sea

Turkey

| 60 | e | 90 | f |
|----|----|----|----|

# Slovenia

**Day One:** *The Julian Alps*

**T**HE MOUNTAIN hut has been opened specially. The climbing and hiking season hasn't yet begun. There is snow all around us, but, more worryingly for our purposes, there is cloud all around us. What should be one of the most spectacular views in the eastern Alps could just as well be someone's back garden. I nurse a mug of herbal tea, personally mixed by our guide. It's a dense, intense brew, a grappa of herbal teas. He spreads his hands apologetically, and looks up at where the sky would probably be if we could see it. It's Slovenia's fault, he says, for being where it is. Moist Mediterranean air is meeting cool, dry air from Central Europe, condensing and covering the monumental landscape like dust-sheets over fine furniture.

There's a map on the wall of the hut and he points out where we are. Almost exactly on the border between Italy and Slovenia, and between what I have grown up to know as Western and Eastern Europe.

For forty-five years of my life the Soviet Union, with its satellite states, had turned half the continent into an alien place; unwelcoming, bureaucratic, grey. For forty-five years Iron Curtains and Cold Wars (sustained for the convenience of both sides) sowed division and mistrust amongst Europeans who should have been friends.

It's been eighteen years now since the fall of the Berlin Wall signalled a new direction for the continent into which I was born. Which is why I'm here 8,000 feet up in the Julian Alps, looking optimistically east, waiting for the cloud to lift so that I can see what the new Europe looks like.

**Right**

*Looking east. The alpine valleys lead down into Slovenia.*

**Opposite**

*Starting out: on the top of the Julian Alps, with Italy behind me and Slovenia ahead.*

**Below**

*Lake Bled and the 1,000 year-old town around it. The church in the middle looks as if it's a ferry crossing the water.*

Two hours later, the clouds start to wither, and we begin to make out solid objects: rocks and boulders peeking out above the snow, the outline of slopes soaring above and below us. Then with a sudden, dizzying effect a final stack of cloud falls off the mountain like an avalanche and the sun strikes buttresses of pink-tinged limestone, cracked and jagged and pointing at the sky. I head off along the path that leads east.

## Day Two: *Bled*

Wake early. Beyond the trees I can see grey light reflected on an eerily still water. Nothing is moving. There is silence apart from the muted chimes of the clock on the church in the middle of the lake, echoed discreetly by a chorus of more distant clocks in the town of Bled.

Villa Bled, where we're staying, is a beautiful, tranquil spot, the sort of place that monks or dictators might choose as a hideaway from the distractions of the world. In this case it was dictators, for this vast pile was built, in 1947, as a getaway for Josip Broz Tito, a.k.a Marshal Tito, one of the giants of post-war communism.

The hotel manager tells me Tito loved Slovenia because it was as far away as he could get from Russia and as close as he could get to Great Britain. Did I know that Elizabeth II had received and decorated him?

The manager shakes her head. 'Unheard of in a communist leader.'

What's more, she gave him a Rolls-Royce, adding to the already impressive stash

**Left**
*The Church of
the Assumption,
Lake Bled. Since
the break-up of
Yugoslavia, the
Catholic Church
is reasserting its
authority in Slovenia.*

of cars given him every Christmas by each grateful country of the Yugoslav Federation. Yugoslavia, generally reckoned to have been one of the more successful creations of post-war communism, never stood much of a chance after the charismatic Tito died in 1980. Slovenia was the first to challenge the system. The walk-out by Slovenian delegates in January 1990 made sure that the 14th Congress of the Yugoslav League of Communists would be the last. Two years and a short war later Slovenian independence was officially recognised.

Walking out this morning I have no sense of Slovenia's communist past. A banner slung across the road announces, in English, that this is the 'Month of Asparagus'. History and religion, two of communism's great enemies, are celebrated everywhere, from the impossibly picturesque Church of the Assumption that sits on an island in the middle of the lake like a carnival float, to the soaring ramparts of the seventeenth-century castle high above the northern shore. The language sounds Germanic, lots of 'Ja Ja's, and the boatmen waiting for tourists are decked out in Tyrolean costume. Houses are of the Alpine style, with overhanging roofs, carved shutters and piles of fresh-cut wood neatly stacked by the doorways. It's not just any sniff of communism that's missing here, it's any sniff of the twentieth century. Bled is in Austro-Hapsburg costume.

I take a ride on the lake with an unsentimental, left-leaning theatre director from the capital, Ljubljana (pronounced Loob-li-Ana). Our *pletna*, a stouter version of a gondola, is punted about by a man called Robert dressed in velvet jacket and pantaloons, with a pole in one hand and a mobile phone in the other. He's clearly more interested in what's happening on the end of the phone.

My companion, Zjelko, whilst not exactly nostalgic, misses the artistic contacts which were so easy during the Yugoslav times. People tend to forget that Slovenia is the most westerly Slav nation in Europe. With a population just short of two million,

the hill from the seafront. Zdravko, the owner, is gregarious and chatty. He introduces me to his son and grandson, both of whom are wearing Arsenal T-shirts.
Fish is the speciality here.

'We always say in Croatia that fish has to swim three times. Sea water, wine and olive oil!' Zdravko enthuses, and a plate of anchovies, sardines and whitebait washed down with a pale pink Croatian rosé is just about faultless.

We talk, inevitably, about the new Croatia.

'I'm very critical, of course,' says Zdravko, 'but imagine living through the fall of communism. It's a fantastic feeling...very emotional.' He doesn't think, however, that Yugoslavia was necessarily doomed and is unusually critical of Marshal Tito.

'You know, the Serbian influence was too strong...especially in his older age. As for your personal human rights there were no limitations, but political expression was cut, harshly. There was no democracy in Yugoslavia and that's why everything fell apart.'

He won't, however, hear any criticism of Croatia's hardline nationalist President Tudjman, who took the country to war in the 1990s and who some think could have stood trial as a war criminal if he'd lived.

'Our President is criticised much more abroad than here...I consider him a real statesman...the father of our country.'

After another bottle of chilled rosé the talk veers towards present-day rivalries. Like the Eurovision Song Contest, taking place tonight. It's already been a small Balkan war of its own, with Serbia and Montenegro withdrawing from the contest because the Serbs accused the Montenegrins of unfairly swinging the vote for their own song. Croatia's hopes lie with Severina, a local girl and a national star. Unfortunately they are not the only things to have lain with Severina. She recently featured in a pornographic video that was broadcast across the country on the internet. Goran shakes his head.

'The day the video was released, nobody worked in Croatia. In the police, in the ministries, in the government, universities, banks, schools.'

'Really?'

'Well, of course there are rare people who say they didn't see it, but I don't trust them at all.'

Later that evening, in a bar by the sea we watch the Eurovision final from Athens. Severina's song, '*Moja Stikla*' ('High Heels'), is loud and bouncy and frenetic and her red skirt, slit to the crotch, is whipped off fairly early in the song. She comes thirteenth.

Croatian pride must have taken a pasting. Not just because she was thirteenth, but because she was soundly beaten by the only two other ex-Yugoslav entrants, Macedonia and Bosnia.

And the bar was half-empty. Perhaps they knew what was going to happen.

**Opposite**
*Stepping out with Goran Golovko in Republic Square, Split's most popular piazza.*

## Day Seven: *Split*

The chief glory of Split is Diocletian's Palace. Not because it is a perfectly preserved and restored example of Roman architecture, but because it's neither of these things. It is a rich, complex, stimulating mess of human settlement, a massive statement of imperial power onto which has been grafted the flotsam and jetsam of centuries of activity and occupation. A city within a city within a city. Lines of washing hang out to dry from the windows of apartments built into the old Roman walls.

Flowers sprout from the top of Corinthian columns, cash tills are embedded in the white limestone walls.

Gaius Aurelius Valerius Diocletianus was a Dalmatian of humble origins who rose through the ranks to become Emperor of Rome for twenty-one years. He acknowledged a division between western and eastern Europe as far back as AD 286 when he divided control of the Roman empire between himself in the east and his friend Maximian in the west, with subordinate 'Caesars' being given control of two other areas. He's had an unfavourable press, partly because in later life he had delusions of divinity, but mostly for his persecution of the Christians. He had, however, an insatiable appetite for new buildings, of which the palace at Split was the most ambitious.

It's a massive structure, part living quarters, part military garrison, measuring 700 by 600 feet with walls 6 feet thick and 25 feet high.

Four great gates give access on each side and it is before the *Mjedna Vrata*, the Bronze Gate, that Goran and I stand this morning. In Diocletian's time ships would have sailed in through here, but access now is from a wide promenade called the Riva.

Inside, in the high-vaulted undercroft where helmets, shields, armour and weapons would once have been unloaded, there is now a busy tourist market selling

**Below**

*Diocletian's Palace,
Split. The peristyle
is the heart of these
massive Roman
remains. The black
granite sphinx is
pre-Christian and the
white bell-tower,
begun in the thirteenth
century, wasn't
finished until 1908.*

postcards, candles, carvings and religious icons (which, considering Diocletian ordered the beheading of Domnius, the patron saint of Split, is a nice irony).

The original layout of the palace, by which all streets lead to the peristyle, the central courtyard, hasn't changed and the square itself is powerful testimony to the skill of Diocletian's masons and builders.

The reign of Diocletian marked the high point of imperial power and the air of invincibility he wanted his mighty palace to project was increasingly tried by Goths, Huns, Avars and others spilling over the eastern borders of the empire. With the Romans gone, the local population used the palace as a refuge and began to build permanent homes inside it. And so it went on. Too big and strong to demolish, successive occupants merely adapted the space, turning it into one of the world's most thriving ruins.

There is a compact horseshoe-shaped bay just below the hotel called Bačvice, its sheltered waters and strip of well worn sand packed with people on this hot weekend. In the shallows a group of men of a certain age are, literally, throwing themselves into a game I've never seen anywhere else. It's called *Picigin*, pronounced Pixigin, and is so local that none of the contestants in the World Championships last year lived anywhere apart from Split. The aim is simple, to keep a tennis ball in the air using any part of the human body, and it's best played in water just above ankle deep, allowing the maximum foot movement and a minimum cushion for the falls. There is only one rule: to keep the ball in the air. Beyond that the game is less about

what you do, than how you do it. Execution is all.

Aerial leaps, back-foot flips, skimming headers, scissor-kicks and wildly reckless full-length falls are all encouraged. Improbably, it was first developed here in the 1920s by a group of academics, journalists, professors and others who were looking for a new form of exercise they could play in the middle of the day. It was very much an anti-club game and one of the first stipulations was that it should be played only on public beaches. Now a group is as likely to include truck drivers as it is night editors. They fling themselves about with enormous good humour, while paddling children scarcely bat an eyelid as middle-aged men come flying through the air. Watching *Picigin* in full flow, I understand better why Yugoslavia was the first non-English-speaking country ever to buy *Monty Python*.

I leave Split on the ferry to the island of Hvar. It's Sunday night and all seats on the deck are taken by a combination of tourists and Hvar-ians returning from a weekend in Split. Cans of beer are ripped open and long-suffering waitresses chatted up. We find some space below in a cabin thick with an old-fashioned fug of cigarette smoke and the sound of gruff voices getting louder by the beer. A game-show plays to nobody on a TV screen in the corner.

Maybe she's just trying to cheer me up, but a bright, intelligent girl, educated on the mainland, but now living back on the island, can't stop raving about the attractions to come. Hvar, she says, is, quite simply, paradise.

## Day Nine: *Hvar*

I find that what catches my fancy most is the smell of the place. Like a slice of Provence cut loose and floated down the Mediterranean, Hvar is famous for its lavender fields. This is not even the lavender season and yet the aromas around me are powerful. The scent of pine mingles with those of broom, dill and oregano, wafting up to me as I stand amongst the stout stone walls of a sixteenth-century hilltop village. Vines are everywhere and each of the courtyards has its own delicately carved winepress.

But the village is deserted and its inhabitants have moved away, to cities like Split or Zagreb or even as far as Australia. My companion and guide Igor Zivanovic loves the island with a vengeance and yet sees that the rural life, however picturesque it might be for visitors like us, offered only hard work and low rewards. Hvar's beauty has never helped its inhabitants. Malta, another Mediterranean island of similar size, sustains a population of 400,000. There are 10,000 living on Hvar.

Igor is what is called in the business a 'character'. He's fifty-one, born in Istria and has lived here since 1961. He wears his long, greying hair in a stumpy ponytail which he is constantly adjusting. Sometimes it's at the back of his head and some-

**Above**
Picigin, *Split's very own beach sport, demands style and shallow water.*

times perched on top of it like a Mandarin emperor. He wears worn jeans and a shirt which pops open rather frequently to reveal a round, bulging stomach.

He has found some donkeys to take us around the deserted village, but even that hasn't been easy. Once the staple form of transport on the island, they have been comprehensively superseded by the motor car and the pick-up truck. Of the two he was able to find, one is lame.

Igor points out the details of the deserted buildings, the carved lintels, decorated keystones on the arches, and the funnel in the millstone on which the wine was pressed.

'They made wine right here. Dark wine. They call it black wine. Very strong.'

Igor dispenses information and opinions with impulsive finality. He doesn't do musing.

In the sleepy little port of Starigrad, on the east side of the island, behind a modest doorway off a winding lane paved with polished slabs of creamy Dalmatian stone, Igor has a *konoba*, a bar/restaurant, which seems to embody his highly individual lifestyle. Marenko, Igor's business partner, is a short, solid Croat with a lined and lived-in face. On his T-shirt is a picture of the Taj Mahal, and underneath it the tortuous slogan 'Via Agra – Man's Greatest Erection for a Woman'.

In the dark cluttered interior Igor is already at work hunting down a bottle of wine. From the ceiling hangs a mobile sculpture on which computer chips are balanced by two books. Plastic hands stick out of an old-fashioned meat grinder. A mannequin's leg is stretched out in a cooler cabinet and there are clocks everywhere, all stopped at 3.04.

'The time Tito died!' shouts Igor from the kitchen. 'He was the greatest hedonist of all time', he adds, approvingly, 'Me, I have to go to the cinema to see Gina Lollobrigida. Tito, he just ring her up.'

The bottle empties quickly and as Igor grabs a corkscrew to open another, Marenko insists I come next door to see something wonderful. It turns out to be a 1904 Swedish-made wall telephone.

Marenko winds it up proudly. 'The oldest telephone set in Croatia.' He hands me the receiver. 'And it still works.'

Sure enough, there is a clear greeting on the end of the line. I reply in English. Much laughter. It obviously happens all the time.

Back at Igor's there seems little sign of the meal, or even a table. Glass in hand, the patron lights another cigarette. 'I hate smoking, but I love cigarettes.' He takes me across to a wall of photos. One shows an emaciated old man apparently being shaved in a public street.

He explains, with unusual warmth of feeling, that this is a man who had been given a day to live and was being given his last shave surrounded by all his friends and neighbours.

**Above**
*The redoubtable Igor.*
*Lover of all things*
*Hvar-ian, especially*
*the wine.*

Our director looks at his watch and mutters something about lunch. Igor makes for the kitchen.

'Come and help me cook,' he shouts behind him, pausing only to point out a bumper sticker from Alaska that reads 'If It's Tourist Season, Why Can't We Shoot Them?'

An hour or so later we are treated to an excellent meal, served on red table mats with hammers and sickles in the corner. Artichoke risotto and polenta, made palatably creamy with butter and oil, freshly caught sardines and a peppery hot lamb stew with *blitva*.

'This is the food of my grandfather and my grandmother,' Igor announces with deep satisfaction, before a familiar theme refuels his anger.

'Tourists! They breed unscrupulous people. People who give them food and take their money without any local people involved at all.' He tips another glass down.

'When McDonald's open here...' He stops, grabs at an imaginary rope round his throat and yanks it upwards.

Back at the villa we're renting I take a dip in the clear, warm waters of a nearby bay. Only when I'm in the water do I become aware that almost every rock below me is covered with sea-urchins.

I swim carefully around and with some skill, though I say it myself, reach a jetty without once having to put a foot down. Am climbing out with a bit of a swagger when a gentle wave propels me forwards and my knee makes contact with a black pincushion. It takes Basil and a razor blade almost half an hour to extract every single quill.

**Above**

*With Igor and the only two donkeys he could find on the island, in one of Hvar's deserted villages. The inhabitants have left to look for work, on the mainland or abroad.*

## Day Eleven: *Hvar to Međugorje, Bosnia & Herzegovina*

At the compact little port of Sućuraj, on the south-eastern tip of Hvar, I leave for the mainland on an equally compact fishing boat. Nets, with their black marker buoys attached to them, lie along the deck like giant jellyfish as we sail out of the harbour beyond the outstretched hand of St Nikolai, patron saint of fishermen, whose statue on the sea wall is, in both senses, the last image of Hvar.

As he rolls the nets out the captain tells me that, contrary to much of the rest of Europe, Croatia's waters are still plentiful. He can bring in 200 kilos a day, but they're mainly scampi, for which the price is low.

'Too many Croatians eat meat,' he grumbles.

The Dalmatian coast, where fish is taken seriously, is eclipsed by Zagreb, the capital, around which half of Croatia's four million people live. And all paid-up carnivores, apparently.

The nets out, our captain produces fresh bread and a dish of anchovies in his own olive oil. He delves around in a locker and brings out a bottle of local wine called Vinka, in a bag of ice. We bob around in the sunshine. The food is simple and satisfying. Ahead of us is the narrow coastal plain and behind it the tall grey limestone wall beyond which are all the troubles of Europe.

By late afternoon we're crossing the Neretva River and turning north through the rich market gardens of its swampy delta into the ancient land of Herzegovina, which, with Bosnia to the north and the Republika Srpska (pronounced Serbska) to the north and east, is one of the components of the fragile state of Bosnia & Herzegovina, or BiH, created and tended by the United Nations.

We pass pillboxes by the railway and further on the minaret of the first mosque I've seen since we set out.

At a border crossing which would not have been here in Yugoslavian days the flag of Croatia with its red chequerboard shield flies alongside Bosnia & Herzegovina's diagonal of stars on a blue and yellow background.

The town that all signs point to is the old Ottoman stronghold of Mostar. The second name on the signs is Međugorje, a village which has become a boom town since six local teenagers had repeated visions of the Virgin Mary. This is to be our stopping place for the night.

Next to our guest house, in the long main street, is an establishment called

'Pilgrimage Specialists' which overflows with candles, crucifixes, rosaries, Virgin Mary baseball hats and mobile phone straps bearing her likeness. Others sell religious art works, like 3D pictures on which the face of Christ changes into the face of the Virgin as you pass by. There are bottles of holy water piled high and statuettes with sparkling lights and lots of walking sticks (whose significance will only become clear later) and establishments called 'Kathy's Irish Kitchen' and 'Paddy Travel'. The main street leads to the twin-towered, cream-painted facade of St James Church, around which are gardens and a fountain and terraces full of people. On this balmy evening they sit or stand, many in groups, quite a lot in wheelchairs. Some are talking quietly, others, hands clasped together, are kneeling in prayer. Others are limping painfully towards the church for mass.

There is such an overwhelming feeling of devotion that writing in my notebook makes me feel like some sort of spy, observing humanity when they are here to observe God.

But I needn't have worried. They're all preoccupied. So rapt that no-one gives me a second glance.

**Above left**
*Igor's eccentric restaurant in Starigrad, Hvar. The slow food is well worth the wait.*

**Above right**
*Another lunch. My fisherman friend checks the wine cellar on the boat to Bosnia.*

# Bosnia & Herzegovina

## Day Twelve: *Međugorje*

In the evening of 24 June 1981, on a rocky hillside above a village of some thousand people in a poor and predominantly Catholic region of Yugoslavia, six young boys and girls encountered a woman with a child in her arms. The next day, four of them, drawn back to the spot, saw the woman again and recognised her as the Virgin Mary. The visitations became a regular, almost daily event for some of the children. Since then, despite no-one else having seen them and even though the Pope has refused to endorse the apparition, twenty-five million pilgrims have visited Međugorje. What was a village has grown into a town of 5,000 inhabitants, with another 20,000 in the area employed in the pilgrimage business. And new hotels are still going up.

Such has been the impact on the local economy that a cynic might think there's a conspiracy to keep a good story going, and when we're suddenly told that one of the original visionaries is happy to meet and talk I wonder if we're using them or they're using us.

Mirjana, a teenager in 1981, is now married to a builder and has two daughters, both of whom are playing table-tennis in the driveway of a comfortable detached house. She is attractive and friendly and as we sit in her eminently sensible garden and she answers my questions eminently sensibly I feel my scepticism, if not destroyed, certainly neutralised. She describes the first vision she had when she was fourteen, apologising only for her English, which is excellent.

'I saw the woman in the grey, long dress and she was carrying the baby, like this, in the hand.'

The next day, accompanied by members of her family, who saw nothing, she once again found herself before the Virgin, who this time spoke to them.

'We come close to the Blessed Mary and she tells us "My dear children, you don't be afraid of me. I am Queen of Peace."'

I press on, with questions I never ever thought I'd hear myself asking.

'Do you still see the Blessed Mary?'

'Yes, every 18th of March. And she also said I will have the apparition every second day of each month.'

'When do you see her?'

'Always about nine o'clock in the morning. But it is not exactly nine o'clock.' She smiles rather apologetically, 'it can sometimes be before or later'.

'D'you have to be somewhere special?'

'I'm always in Cenacolo.' She points up the road to a drug rehabilitation centre we'd passed on the way here, built by her husband's company and run by a well funded order of nuns.

The fact that Mirjana, someone whose visions have spawned an industry, appears to be no hysteric or wild-eyed prophetess but an ordinary housewife, leaves me feeling somehow cheated.

Later in the afternoon, back in Međugorje, I hear Ivan, the only one of the visionaries to whom Mary still appears on a daily basis, talking to an enormous crowd in one of the great purpose-built pavilions behind the church. He speaks softly into the microphone, like a comfortable Californian businessman, in a pale blue polo shirt and jeans, his long hair brushed neatly back. It's as if these extraordinary people have worked hard to look and sound as ordinary as possible.

This being the Balkans, there is, of course, a political dimension. The message of Međugorje is for Catholics only, and the power of this whole operation reflects what has happened to the Balkans since the break-up of Yugoslavia. Catholics have always been the majority here in Herzegovina, but at the time of the Ottoman empire they lived alongside Muslims. Now nationalism is in the air and new countries like Croatia and Serbia define themselves

**Below**

*In Međugorje I talk to Mirjana, one of the children who saw the Virgin Mary, and who still does.*

not by what they have in common with their neighbours but what makes them different. Thousands of Catholics have moved down here from elsewhere in Bosnia to avoid living with Muslims, making Međugorje, which offers such comfort to pilgrims from all over the world and which preaches the Virgin's message of peace, into another symbol of the new polarisation.

Whilst we're filming in the main street an old car drives up aggressively in our shot and two heavy-set men get out, slamming the doors. I notice a tag hanging from the mirror. It says 'Heroes' on one side, and on the other is the name and likeness of Ante Gotovina, a Croatian general now under indictment at The Hague for war crimes. The EU had made his capture a condition of talks on Croatian membership.

At sunset we follow a long line of pilgrims up to Apparition Hill where Mirjana, Ivan and their two friends first saw the Virgin. It's not an easy walk and many have to negotiate the rugged path with the help of sticks. The spot where she first appeared is marked by a white statue with fencing around, set in a rough stony area dotted with pomegranate trees and thorn-bush scrub. Some sit or kneel in quiet contemplation around this sacred place but as I draw close to the statue I hear a broad Irish accent whispering in my ear.

'Which way for the crosses, now Michael?' and mistaking my wide-eyed amazement for confusion, the voice adds, helpfully,

'*Life of Brian*, my favourite film!'

**Above**
*On Apparition Hill, Međugorje, pilgrims pray at the spot where the Virgin first appeared to the six children.*

Though he can remember only one fatality from diving, twenty-three members of the club died in the war of 1993.

The area around the bridge has been well restored, with the inevitable cobbled streets and orderly tidied-up markets, but you only have to climb up into the back streets to see the extent of the war damage. Burnt-out hulks of buildings pitted with shrapnel, the windows of the Union Bank building smashed and the gouges of pre-stressed concrete still hang down the walls. A richly decorated Hapsburg-style building that used to be Mostar's best hotel is roofless and empty.

Kamel, who lived through the siege, who ran for water for his family at the risk of his life, refused to be bowed. He taught himself English and worked as a runner for the UN force that saved the city. Now they've gone he's retrained into computers.

He thinks it will be a long time before Mostar can once again become the prosperous, tolerant, lively city it once was. Many people who could be helping to rebuild it have left and gone abroad, and the tripartite Croat, Muslim and Serb administration of Bosnia & Herzegovina, with its colonial-style, EU-appointed High Representative is a reminder that of all the countries of the Balkans, this is perhaps the most serious casualty of war.


## Day Fourteen: *Mostar to Sarajevo*

Mostar railway station, from which we hope to travel to Sarajevo, is a sad, neglected place. The platforms are functional and bare. The 'M' of Mostar is missing from the only sign and wild flowers sprout from the track.

There are so few people waiting that my belief in the existence of the eight o'clock to Sarajevo is diminishing by the minute. But, bang on time, I see a headlamp beaming out of the tunnel and the metallic green diesel locomotive and three coaches that comprise the Ploče to Zagreb express squeal to a halt beside us.

The compartments are comfortable enough but give off the dusty, sweaty smell of stock that is often used but rarely cleaned. Once we're on the move north what we lack in creature comforts is more than made up for by some fine scenery as we follow the Neretva into a narrow gorge with dramatic walls of twisted, folded rock.

A Bosnian-Croat army officer is travelling up to Sarajevo. His face is like one of the Easter Island statues, long, with protruding eyebrows and a big, firm jaw. His eyes and his hair are both deep black and he learnt his English whilst training in

Texas. He's another who talks admiringly of Marshal Tito and the skill with which he played off West and East.

'Technology from US and Europe, arms from Russia.'

He regards him as a visionary, a man who genuinely tried to create a third force in politics by allying himself with people like Nehru of India.

'I cried when he died,' he says. 'Nowadays everyone says, "I didn't cry. He was a butcher." But I cried.'

Alongside us, as the valley widens, trout farms and ageing hydroelectric plants make use of the river. My soldier friend shakes his head at their condition.

'But what can you do. Over fifty per cent of our qualified people have gone abroad.'

'Do they come back?'

He laughs. 'In the summer!'

I can see why you might want to come back in the summer. As we run deeper into the heart of the Dinaric Alps the scenery is magnificently wild and romantic, sometimes tight and confined by rock stacks and perilous buttresses, then suddenly opening out into a vista of lakes with houses by the water and gardens of beehives and orchards.

As the Romans used roads, the Austrians used railways to cement their empire. They were impressive engineers. Of the 80 miles of line between Mostar and Sarajevo, forty per cent is in tunnels and ten per cent on bridges or viaducts.

The Ivan Tunnel, cutting through 3,000-foot-high mountains, was so difficult to drill that the Emperor Franz Josef, rather rashly, urged on the workforce with the promise of 'one kilo of gold for one kilo of stone'. It marks the end of Herzegovina and the beginning of Bosnia. The weather has completely changed from one end of the tunnel to the other and the sunny skies that we've been blessed with since setting out from Slovenia have been replaced by dark and scowling clouds.

Not the best conditions for a first glimpse of Sarajevo, which presents a grimly bleak aspect as we trundle through an industrial wasteland bordered by tall concrete blocks broken up by scrapyards and factories that look derelict until you see people moving about. This, I later learn, is what they call New Sarajevo.

We walk from the station to the Holiday Inn, a squat concrete core from which hangs a skin of yellow and brown tiles. It was built for the Winter Olympics of 1984 and still bears the Olympic symbol on its side. The nearby shell of the multi-storey Parliament building is a reminder of more recent history, the nightmare of the 1990s, when Sarajevo lived under bombardment for almost four years.

**Above**

*With the fast-flowing Neretva River below, Mostari divers, members of one of the most elite dangerous sports clubs in the world, leap 70 feet into 15 feet of water.*

I can feel the first flecks of rain.

In a comfortable, elegantly appointed restaurant off a dusty street I meet a group of Sarajevans who all work in films, television or journalism: Ademir, a film director and producer, Glava, a bearded heavily built Serb who's just written a comedy screenplay, and Srdjan (imagine 'Sir John' in an American accent), also a writer and director. They're full of plans for future projects, but, as a newcomer in town, I can't help asking about the past.

Srdjan sighs. Sarajevans today don't want to talk about the war. But once they start they can't stop. Ademir, tall, thin, with a strong, ascetic face, is the oldest of the men and Bosnia's most respected film maker. He was one of the few who managed to get in and out of the city during the siege.

'The only way was on a plane. They were operated by Germans, Americans and French. We called them Maybe Airlines. Maybe the plane would take off, maybe not.'

**Above**

*On the Mostar-Sarajevo train, through the Dinaric Alps. Almost half the line is in tunnels as it cuts through the mountains.*

Boarding call was a shout or a gesture followed by a sprint out to the aircraft, carrying all your own bags and wearing an improvised UN flak jacket.

The next thing he knew he was in Cannes or San Francisco. 'It was hard to get out, but so much harder to come back. To come from the world like that to a city without electricity, telephone, running water.' He shakes his head as though he still can't comprehend it.

He's bitter about the siege, but reserves his anger equally for Serbia's President Milosevic and the system that allowed him to do what he did and the countries of the West that ignored the plight of Sarajevo for so long.

Then I make the mistake of trying to make instant sense of all this.

'But there's still a Serbian republic within Bosnia & Herzegovina,' I ask with innocent surprise.

Looks are exchanged. Glava explains.

'What do you mean "still"? There has been and always will be a Serb part of Bosnia. It's like asking the Protestants in Belfast why there's still a place called Northern Ireland.'

On the streets of Sarajevo, there's a lively, comfortable bustle, the feel of a city going about its business. It was always the focal point of the Balkans, a place where travellers and traders on their way between Central Europe and the Mediterranean and Western Europe and the East met and mingled, and it remained cosmopolitan and tolerant during the Ottoman occupation. Srdjan reminds me that there was a thriving Jewish community here, with much greater freedom from persecution than almost anywhere else in Europe. A walk through the centre of Sarajevo, he says, is a walk through time, from the old Turkish quarter, through the imperious Art Nouveau facades of the Austro-Hapsburg centre to the Tito-era communist blocks in the west.

As in Mostar, mosques and churches seem to have been restored as a matter of priority and in one square, within a hundred yards of each other, can be found a synagogue, a Catholic church, an Orthodox church, a mosque and a Seventh Day Adventists' meeting hall.

I take a tram back to the hotel. The tramline runs along what was known in the war as Sniper Alley, a place you crossed at your peril. As I step down I look up towards the hills from which the snipers operated with such impunity. They look green, inviting, almost idyllic, dotted with red-roofed villas and bungalows. Only a dozen years ago they were dangerous, malignant places from which the Serb artillery looked down on the city like an audience at a theatre.

Over 11,000 died in the siege of Sarajevo. Ademir says that it took a long time after the war before he could look up at these beautiful mountains without flinching.

## Day Fifteen: *Sarajevo*

In the suburb of Butmir, at the house of the Kolar family, is a display headed 'Sarajevo Olympic City 1984, Surrounded City 1992–1995'. It's not absolutely accurate. The fact that Sarajevo survived the siege at all was because it was never quite surrounded. There was one way in and out, and it was through the Kolar house.

In June 1992 the UN struck an agreement with the Bosnian Serb leader Ratko Mladic to keep Sarajevo airport open for humanitarian aid. This in theory offered a break in the chain of encirclement, except that the UN had also agreed with Mladic that no Bosnians should be allowed in the airport perimeter. After some 800 people had died trying to get across, the poorly armed Bosnian army defending the city turned in desperation to a tunnel beneath the airport.

**Above**
*A wet day in Sarajevo. Rebuilding of mosques (like the one in the background) and churches was given priority in post-war reconstruction.*

It was cramped, the average width and height throughout its 880-yard length being no more than four and a half feet. It was frequently under water and twice flooded to the ceiling, but it enabled supplies of food, medicine, ammunition and human reinforcements to be moved in and out. A small railway was constructed and eventually telephone cables and a rudimentary oil pipeline were also fed through. It's estimated that this tiny artery beneath the airport saved 300,000 lives.

The house, still bearing the scars of bombardment, is now open as a museum, presided over by Bajro and Edis Kolar. Edis can't be far off thirty but like others I've met in Sarajevo he has the world-weary air of a much older man. His lightly tinted spectacles, soft voice and matter-of-fact delivery give him the abstracted air of a put-upon teacher, but during the war, when in his teens, he was part of a crack military unit whose job it was to select and take out Serbian artillery posts.

'I was a war veteran at the age of twenty-one.' He laughs ruefully.

He remembers walk-ins of over fourteen hours, with full equipment and often in darkness.

'I saw many things that most people will never see in their whole life.'

At the back of the Kolar house is a scene of rural serenity. Rows of beans, spring onions and potatoes, groves of walnut trees and apple orchards grow where the tunnel used to run. Beyond them, almost up against the perimeter fence, I can see a woman in a headscarf, tilling the soil by hand whilst behind her a red airport radar scanner circles the skies. She doesn't look up as one of the only two flights of the morning roars up and away from Sarajevo.

Only about 100 feet of tunnel remains, but small parties of tourists are constantly calling. There are hardly any visitors from Bosnia.

'They don't want to remember', says Edis. 'But they always will.'

Anywhere with a Hapsburg and Ottoman pedigree will have its fair share of cafés but in central Sarajevo you are never more than 20 yards away from a cup of coffee. Nor do you have to go far to find delightful buildings, like the restful, soothing, wood-scented, sensitively restored Serbian Orthodox church in Mula Mustafa Bašeskija. Despite being Serbian it was the first church to be shelled, and once the Serbs retreated it was the first to be rebuilt. In the Turkish quarter there are stone-built minarets and domes which remind me how graceful Islamic architecture can be. In narrow Sarači Street near the old Turkish market eight elegant stone chimneys with conical lead coverings rise above an old library.

Just outside the Old Town the streets open onto a wide esplanade, built by the Austrians and lining either side of the Miljacka River. The flow moves sluggishly

**Right**

*The house of the Kolar family, beneath which the only tunnel to break the siege of Sarajevo was dug, still bears the scars of war.*

**Left**
*Inside a restored
section of the tunnel.
An average of 4,000
people used it each day
for over two years.*

through, its thin stream dribbling over a series of low weirs, in each of which a bobbing jetsam of plastic bottles and beer cans collects, turning and tumbling ceaselessly.

Beside a bridge above this modest stream is, both literally and figuratively, one of the great turning points of history. On an easily missed stone plaque set low in an anonymous wall are the words (in Bosnian and English) 'From this place on 28th June 1914 Gavrilo Princip assassinated the heir to the Austro-Hungarian throne Franz Ferdinand and his wife Sofia.' Had Franz Ferdinand's coach not stopped here that day and presented Princip with a sitting target, because of the coachman's confusion as to whether to turn into the town or continue along the embankment, the First World War might never have begun. Well, might never have begun just here.

We eat tonight with Ademir, his wife Selma and friends at a traditional restaurant hung with antiques which overlooks the city. An enormous spread of Bosnian goodies including a light and subtle ravioli with yoghurt, intensely tasty little lamb and beef sausages called *ćevapi*, pitta bread and fresh onions, potato pie, spinach pie and spit-roasted lamb. We talk of many things and there is much laughter. Bosnians pride themselves on their sense of humour. For many, jokes were an essential way of dealing with the pain of war.

Unlike the Croatians.

'In Zagreb', I'm assured, 'they don't like to laugh.'

Then two guitarists and an eighty-one-year-old accordionist serenade us, which would be a bit of an intrusion were it not for the accompanying voice of a dark-haired forty-year-old called Almira, who sings in what they call *sevdalinka* style, gliding softly into their rhythms, her voice poised delicately on the edge of sadness and elation.

**Above**

*A bridge over the thin stream of the Miljacka River. The green hills beyond look pleasant now but the Serb army sat up there and shelled the city for more than three years.*

It's beautiful and haunting. I ask her if she trained as a singer. 'No, I trained as an accountant.'

Recovering from this blow to my romantic imagination I ask Almira if she can describe the Bosnian character. Her dark eyes narrow and she replies without a pause. 'We are stubborn, passionate, impulsive. That's always our problem. But we enjoy our life.'

Whatever has happened here before, I feel very much at ease in Sarajevo.

## Day Sixteen: *Sarajevo*

'We have found four anti-tank mines and one anti-personnel just in the bush area over there, so it's a live minefield. Stay within the marked area. Do not go through the tapes. Keep your helmet on at all times.'

We're less than a mile to the west of Vrelo Bosne, one of Sarajevo's most popular picnic spots, where tables are set beneath overhanging willow trees and horse-drawn carriages can be hired by the hour.

There are no horse-drawn carriages where we are. There are pick-up trucks and four-wheel drives, an ambulance, men with helmets and visors and sniffer dogs. The woods and meadows are ringed with red and white police tape and marked with skull and crossbone signs. This is poisoned country, one of Bosnia's many mine-fields. If you picnic here you could be killed.

'If something happens, do not run, just stay put. There is medical support in place. If something happens they will help you out of the minefield still alive.'

With a disarming grin, Damir, a strong, stocky ex-soldier who's in charge of this clearance operation, brings our briefing to an end, jabs his head towards the fields and beckons us to follow. I'm wearing a flak jacket and helmet, but somehow that just makes me feel more vulnerable, as if something really could go wrong out there. All of us have had to sign disclaimer forms and fill in our blood groups.

We set off along an avenue of blue and white plastic tape. On one side, up the slope, the field has been shaved almost down to the bare earth; on the other side, the uncut grass of the valley floor is threaded with a profusion of blue, red and yellow wild flowers – buttercups, gentian, daisies.

Further up the hill, and half-hidden in the undergrowth, are the shells of good-sized suburban houses destroyed in the war, with stalks of cow parsley nodding through the holes where the windows used to be.

Damir tells me that there are limited funds available for mine-clearance and open countryside, however beautiful, comes way down the list of priorities. His work is paid for by the Norwegian government, and there are many other international donors they depend on.

'But the Balkans is off the TV now. There is Iraq and Darfur and…well, Bosnia is not such a big thing any more.'

I ask Damir about the sort of mines he has to deal with. The Prom-1, 'the bounding one', he says, is particularly nasty.

It turns out to be a device, activated by either tripwires or foot pressure, which, on detonation, jumps out of the ground, and a second charge explodes in the air.

'It's the most dangerous mine you can find in the field, and both my colleagues got killed by that type.'

'You've lost two colleagues?'

He nods. 'Just a moment's lapse in concentration.'

I flinch at the sound of a distant roar as we round the side of the hill. It comes from an adjacent patch to the one we're working on. A remote-controlled vehicle with flailing chains in front of it is doing the primary clearance, ripping out saplings and bushes to prepare the ground for the second stage, the 'gardening work', as

**Below**
*Two faces of Sarajevo, surely the most resilient city in modern Europe.*

Damir calls it. This involves meticulous scrutiny, using metal detectors first then painstakingly slow hands-and-knees examination to search for tell-tale signs like tripwires or antennae. 'And all the landmines are green. Makes things really difficult.'

Only after this work is done are the dogs brought in. They can detect explosive which might have been missed deep beneath the surface (my mind can't help going back to truffle-hunting in Istria).

We watch the dogs work, leading their handlers slowly up the hill alongside a strip of marker tape. The best dogs for mine detection, says Damir, are Belgian Shepherds, though some use German Shepherds or Labradors. Fortunately the stretch is clear, but to show us how the dogs react Damir plants a tiny amount of TNT a few inches down. When the dog encounters it, she actually points down at it with her nose, then sits back on her haunches, gazing proudly up at the handler who marks the spot.

Damir tells me that most of the de-mining teams are made up of ex-military. In many cases those doing clearing are the ones who planted the mines in the first place.

He defends them. Mine-laying was a military tactic, used in war to defend positions and kill enemy infantry who might otherwise kill you. He fought for the Bosnian government army in the war and laid mines himself.

'And at that time you do not think about consequences for civilians. At that time you think about your own life and how to protect yourself. During the conflict we did not think what would happen in Bosnia afterwards.'

Now they're paying a big price. Some of the devices, especially the Yugoslav-made 'bounding' mines are particularly well made and won't deteriorate.

'They don't get old, they just sit and wait.'

We walk back through some of the most beautiful unspoilt natural meadowland I've seen anywhere in Europe. In England this would be a nature reserve. In Bosnia it's a lethal problem.

**Opposite**
*Meeting one of the
mine-clearing dogs in
the potentially deadly
fields outside Sarajevo.*

## Day Seventeen: *Sarajevo to Dubrovnik*

I linger at the window of my hotel room one last time, trying to collect together my memories of this extraordinary place. More than in any other city I find it hard to take in Sarajevo without my imagination running the past and present in parallel. I can't look at the road without seeing people racing for dear life across it, I can't look to the broad green mountain slopes without seeing lines of gun barrels pointing back at me. I can't see the shell of the Parliament building opposite without thinking I can hear the whizz and thump of rockets and mortars.

I'm shocked at how the city suffered only a dozen years ago and inspired by how they've come out of it. I also know now that most Sarajevans I've talked to would feel uncomfortable at any suggestion of saintly suffering. They feel they shouldn't have got into the mess they did but they also feel irritated by the crocodile tears of foreigners whose governments let one of Europe's great cities be slowly strangled. Life goes on, is about all one can say as we pack our vehicles up, dodging the stream of taxis and minibuses delivering new guests. Life goes on. Cities heal quickly.

It's very different in the countryside. As the road winds south-east, the aftermath of war is much less easy to disguise. Blasted and blackened shells of buildings can be glimpsed between the trees.

A half-hour outside Sarajevo, signs by the roadside remind us of new enmities. Written now in Cyrillic as well as Roman script, they advise us that we are entering the Republika Srpska, a self-governing entity within the Republic of Bosnia & Herzegovina, which represents the country's 1.36 million Serbs (along with some two million Muslims and 750,000 Croats).

The comparative harmony that's been restored in Sarajevo seems markedly absent here. This is a hardline heartland. Ratko Mladic, leader of the army that squeezed the life out of Sarajevo for three years and hero of the Bosnian Serbs, is from this pretty valley. Local police, in ill-fitting uniforms, with caps pushed back on their heads, wave us down and check our driver's licence. Then, just as I'm beginning to simplify all this into a clear case of heroes and villains, we meet up with a Serbian group of actors and entertainers who believe so strongly in a multi-ethnic Bosnia that they spend their time touring schools in confrontational areas like this.

They call themselves Genesis and they come from Banja Luka, the capital of Republika Srpska, 200 miles away to the north-west. Diana, the driving force behind the group, is a big, dynamic girl with spiky blond hair and tightly stretched pink pants. We follow her to a school in Trnovo (pronounced Turnovo) where today, helped and encouraged by UNICEF, the United Nations Children's Fund, she and her team are to present their 45-minute puppet show, teaching the children co-existence, tolerance and how not to be killed by landmines.

The school is in pretty bad shape. It's barely recovered from being hit by NATO planes, which after three years' vacillation finally began their attack on Serb positions in 1995. It was built for 600 children, but now only 120 attend. Many young families couldn't wait for the firing to stop before moving away from Trnovo, leaving behind a ghost town whose population is predominantly over sixty-five.

For Diana and Genesis this is the sort of challenge they relish. They've bussed in thirty Bosniak children from a nearby school to swell the audience and to mix the communities. They all get on fine, the way children do.

And the show is terrific. It takes the form of a trial and the judge asks the children to be the jury. Up pops a landmine, a green puppet with mad-staring eyeballs, sharp teeth and a long yellow neck. This is followed by a grenade, which arrives with a very realistic whizz and explosion. A fat friendly Bumble Bee is especially popular with the children. He tells them that landmines can be moved by water, relevant in a country that has so many rivers and streams. Cat has brought Mouse before the court because he has a gun in his house. The children are encouraged to tell Mouse all the things that are wrong with playing with a pistol.

It's all done with noise and energy, and for a grim subject, a great deal of humour. The children sit entranced.

The good news from Diana is that the rate of accidents from mines is falling each year. In 2005 there were nineteen victims throughout BiH, so far in 2006 eight people have been killed and four seriously wounded. The bad news is she reckons it will be seventy years before they can safely till every field and pick herbs in every forest again.

As we drive south and east we enter the increasingly wild and desolate landscape of the Trebišnjica valley. The rain pours down from a big, black threatening sky and the settlements become increasingly few and far between. At a roadside restaurant surrounded by low gnarled pine scrub our arrival stirs a big dog, as black as the sky, to a fury of barking and clanging as it twists and turns in its chains.

The weather and the scenery become even more apocalyptic as the mountains rise around us and the cloud and rain thicken. It's night by the time we reach the Republika Srpska border and a few hundred yards further on the red chequer flag announces our return to Croatia.


# Croatia

**Day Nineteen:** *Dubrovnik*

As the crow flies, Sarajevo and Dubrovnik are less than 90 miles apart, but their outward and visible appearances could hardly be more different. In Sarajevo the scars of war are plain to see, whereas her southern neighbour gleams and glitters as if freshly polished. Yet one of the first things that confronts you as you walk through Ploče Gate into the immaculate Old Town is a large map showing that even 'the jewel of the Adriatic' was not spared the violence that convulsed the Balkans.

Beneath the heading 'City Map of Damages Caused by the Aggression on

Dubrovnik by the Yugoslav Army – Serbs and Montenegrins – 1991–1992' is a pattern of coloured dots and triangles analysing the bombardment in minute detail. 'Roofs damaged by direct impact', 'Houses burned,' 'Roofs damaged by shrapnels' and even 'Direct impact on pavement'. You would probably need a map the size of a football pitch to record the damage sustained by Sarajevo, but the fact remains that, in the eyes of the West, the two great outrages of the war were the destruction of the bridge at Mostar and the shelling of Dubrovnik.

Dubrovnik, or Ragusa as it was known until 1918, was always a magnet for visitors. The stout sixteenth-century walls were designed by Italian architects to protect merchants and traders and to rival the power and glory of Venice, their aggressive competitor to the north. So when the mortar shells, specifically targeting the historic old town, began falling in November 1991, it was not only an affront to her dignity, it was major threat to her livelihood.

Branka Franicevic, now a tour guide, was in her thirties when it all happened and we talk together outside a *kavana* (café) in the *Stradun*, the long, paved street that runs the length of the Old City.

She remembers the morning of the very first hit. 'I believed that nobody normal, at the end of the twentieth century, could shell a town like Dubrovnik', she recalls. 'Then I heard a very strange sound. I thought maybe I had turned in my dream, but my mother came and forced me to go to the cellar of the house, and the first thing that happened was my neighbour who came with a glass of cognac and a cigarette.'

From then on it was not the shells falling that was the worst thing, but the cutting of the water and electricity supplies. 'For five months we were permitted only five litres of water per family per day.' Six centuries after they were built the great stone fortresses guarding the city became sanctuaries once again.

'In the Revelin fortress at the east gate, 2,000 people moved in and spent nine months with only one toilet. And, interesting, no diseases, nothing like that.'

**Below**
*Dubrovnik at dawn. Known for most of its life as Ragusa, the city rivalled Venice as one of the most powerful trading ports of the Mediterranean.*

**Opposite**
Stradun. *Dubrovnik. The fine limestone paved main street that runs the length of the old city. Always busy when the cruise ships are in.*

**Left**
*Coffee with my guide Branka, at a Stradun-side café.*

One thing of which there was no shortage was *rakija*, a potent herb brandy.

'It added to the spirits of the locals,' recalls Branka, with a trace of an apologetic smile. They had big meals, sang and danced a lot, enjoyed discussing what they might do if the Serbs tried to enter the city – boiling olive oil was considered – and generally had such a good time that when the war ended with the tourist business in terminal decline, Branka felt a perverse relief.

'I felt I had been given my city back.'

Frightening though it must have been to have 2,000 shells lobbed, with fiendish arbitrariness, into such a confined area, nothing here came close to the suffering inflicted on Sarajevo. Within months of the siege being lifted, seventy per cent of the roofs were relaid, the stonework was patched up and Dubrovnik was back in business.

As if to illustrate the point, a tidal wave of tourists pours through the Pile Gate, the western entrance to the Old Town, and within minutes the *Stradun* is filled with wall-to-wall sightseers.

Branka and many other locals feel that it is the cruise ships that are over-whelming the old town. From one vessel alone, up to 2,500 visitors can spill into the narrow streets, spending, as she points out, an average of only 13 euros each, whereas those staying in hotels and pensions on land spend over 100 each. There is pressure from many who love the old city to limit the size of the ships in order to preserve its character. This may be one of the very few instances of a city legislating against its own appeal, but Dubrovnik/Ragusa has an honourable and progressive tradition of civic pride. The writer Dervla Murphy notes that the city introduced Europe's first garbage collection, a drinking water system with fines for pollution, abolished torture in the seventeenth century, the slave trade in the fifteenth century and never allowed the Inquisition within its walls. They have had pedestrianisation for hundreds of years. Rationing tourists shouldn't be beyond this redoubtable city.

A torrential downpour clears the streets more effectively than any legislation, leaving the *Stradun*'s shiny smooth paving – limestone from the island of Korčula, a dozen miles away to the north-west – glistening in fresh sunshine.

Later I swim in a cool Adriatic with smells of grilling fish wafting out from the shore and a hazy lemon sunset replacing the baleful clouds of yesterday.

## Day Twenty: *Dubrovnik*

'Those who seek Paradise on earth should come to Dubrovnik', wrote George Bernard Shaw, in one of his comparatively rare tourist endorsements. I think of this today as, on my way to the hotel breakfast room, I hear a plaintive Yorkshire voice drifting up from the back stairs.

'I'm lost.'

Another, equally Yorkshire voice, only male this time, shouts down.

'Which floor are you after, love?'

'Minus One.'

Nowhere is far from anywhere else in the old walled city and, only a few yards away from cruiseliner land, complete peace and tranquillity can be enjoyed in the cloister of the Franciscan priory, where we gather to listen to a Bosnian-born lute player called Edin, so expert at his craft that he has just come from working with Sting on a recording of the work of the English lutenist and contemporary of Shakespeare, John Dowland.

The courtyard is intimate and attractive, criss-crossed with aromatic box hedge, oleander, bougainvillea and palm and fruit trees. The arches of the cloister are simple and elegant, of pale stone in slender double columns, but it's the elaborate, well-restored capitals that catch the eye, including one which they say depicts the architect himself, Mihoje Brajkov, his jaw swollen with the toothache he was suffering at the time. The man clearly had a sense of humour as it is grotesque creatures, human caricatures and wild beasties that dominate rather than angels and disciples. He died in 1348, of the plague they called the Black Death, which raged through Europe, killing one-third of the population.

Edin could be a latter-day Brajkov. He's extraordinarily skilful and has a deadpan humour. His big face is dominated by wide, eloquent eyes and he's constantly worrying away at an undisciplined fringe of floppy black hair.

'I have to have it cut,' he says apologetically. 'I look like a Bosnian bus driver.'

I learn from him that the lute was first mentioned in the seventh century, in Syria, where the instrument was called *al oud*, which came to Europe through Spain, became *la oud* and eventually 'lute'. The one he's playing today has fourteen strings and dates from 1600. Wanting to avoid any Golden Hits syndrome, Edin tests himself with an adaptation of Bach's Toccata and Fugue, originally written for the organ.

He frowns as he adjusts his fingers.

'It's difficult. They have two hands and two feet.'

The result is lovely and technically dazzling, and even when one of the strings snaps it seems to snap in time with the music.

'Is there anything you can play without the string?'

**Left**
*Bosnian Edin
Karamazov, a top
lute player who has
recorded with Sting,
still enjoys busking
in Dubrovnik.*

Edin frowns, nods and goes into a perfect rendition of 'Over the Rainbow'.

His star is in the ascendant now as people discover an instrument whose popularity seemed to have been on the wane since the days of Mozart.

'I play in concert halls, but there is no place like here, where I can play outside. In Dubrovnik you can do anything. In Venice police is everywhere, everything is controlled. Here you can do anything you want.'

To mark our last night in Dubrovnik we end up at a jazz bar down by the old port. The band is augmented every now and then by a Gérard Depardieu lookalike who rolls out of the bar behind them, launches into thunderous versions of the jazz classics and disappears back in for a top-up.

I'm told I'll get to know him well over the next couple of days. He's the captain of our boat to Albania.

## Day Twenty-one: *Dubrovnik to Durrës*

Our boat may be called 'Adriatic Paradise' but Captain Neven (I never find out his surname), admits that there are problems. One is that he's never been to Albania before.

'Perhaps only fifty Croatians ever have gone there.'

The other is that he doesn't want to go and can't really understand why anyone else would.

Having established that, he's friendly enough and points out various interesting features along the way. As we leave the harbour we pass an elegant suspension bridge supported by a fan of grey steel cables. There had, apparently, been much political controversy over the naming of the bridge. The left wanted to call it the

**Right**

*Time to leave
Dubrovnik to the
cruise-ships.*

Dubrovnik Bridge, the right wanted to call it, after their nationalist President, the Franjo Tuđman Bridge. After long and bitter argument a compromise was reached and it is now called the Dubrovnik Bridge of Franjo Tuđman. Captain Neven, wild of hair and round of stomach, chuckles loudly as he tells me this.

We have a fine last view of the ramparts of old Dubrovnik on one side and on the other the offshore island of Lokrum. The Hapsburg Archduke Maximilian decided to turn the monastery on the island into a summer residence for himself and his wife. The locals knew that no good would come of this and they were right. Maximilian later accepted the title of Emperor of Mexico, where he was shot by firing squad in 1867. His wife went mad. Crown Prince Rudolf ignored local superstition and chose the island for his honeymoon. A few years later he committed suicide after shooting dead his mistress.

But it does have a nudist beach.

The crew of 'Adriatic Paradise' is an odd bunch, consisting of two slightly surly men in their late thirties, and a mysterious and glamorous woman in a low-cut dress, high heels and a black straw hat who we assume is the waitress/hostess we were promised.

'She is Nada,' says the captain, which seems a bit hard, until we realise that this is her name.

At lunchtime she fixes some beers, but totally ignores us after that and spends the afternoon out on deck taking more and more clothes off until she's wearing only her black straw hat. None of us dares ask her for a cup of coffee.

Captain Neven sits behind the wheel, usually on his mobile phone. He's from Zagreb, the Croatian capital, and spends the summer running a boat charter company with his brother and the winter singing in musicals and light opera. Last year he was Judas in the Zagreb production of *Jesus Christ Superstar*, which had a fifteen-day run. This is apparently quite good for a foreign musical sung in Croatian.

**Left**
*Our hostess on the*
*Adriatic Paradise.*
*No-one dared ask her*
*for a cup of coffee.*

In the former Yugoslavia there were much better prospects for shows like this, he says, when five countries shared a language and there was five times the potential audience.

In the afternoon a rubber dinghy, which doubles as the ship's lifeboat, is commandeered for Nigel to take some shots of the 'Adriatic Paradise' in full sail. Unfortunately the dinghy is half-full of stagnant seawater, which, as it's dragged over the side, spills through an open porthole and onto a suitcase of fresh, clean clothes, which an hour later I discover are mine.

Meanwhile the task of raising the sails proves impossible and the shot is abandoned.

The captain glowers at the crew and takes it out on Albania.

'Albania is for us like some kind of black hole,' he scowls. 'There is no need to go there and for them I think the same.'

I try to tell him it's the secrecy and isolation that attract me to the country, but he isn't impressed by such romantic nonsense.

It's clear, even at this late stage, that the captain will try anything to avoid going to Albania. He suggests at one point that we should put into Montenegro to see their independence celebrations. (On Thursday last week they voted in a referendum to secede from Serbia, making them Europe's newest country, despite a population little bigger than that of Sheffield.) There should be a good party, he says, the Montenegrins being famously lazy.

He recovers his natural ebullience over a glass or two and as the sun quietly sets, cooks us a superb mussel risotto with Turkish spices – 'Croatians don't like to use spices' – and becomes very jolly and relaxed.

Later I lie down below deck in my hot little cabin with both ports open and the only sound I can hear above the hammer-blow thudding of the engine is the captain, singing at the top of his voice.

**Above**

*Neven, opera singer, captain, cook, takes a sunset supper with me on the* Adriatic Paradise *as Montenegro, the newest country in Europe, slips by on the horizon.*

## Day Twenty-two: *Dubrovnik to Durrës*

When I wake up the dawn has barely broken. The coastline, indistinct in detail at this early hour, is lower and gentler than the tall grey cliffs of Croatia.

There's nothing Homeric about the 'Adriatic Paradise' this morning. Nada and the other two crew members are nowhere to be seen. Captain Neven is strapped to the wheel, fast asleep, rolling gently to and fro with the swell. I look anxiously ahead and wonder whether to wake him up as we're heading straight for a small island.

Two hours later, we've made ourselves some breakfast and the captain is now awake, standing at the wheel and talking animatedly into his mobile while casting anxious looks at the coast ahead.

The city of Durrës, Albania's chief port, slides into view to the south-east, between green hills covered with vines, golden-flowered broom and communications masts. Missing are the red-roofed whitewashed houses which helped make the towns and villages of the Croatian coast look attractive, but Durrës looks busy, with big modern blocks and builders' cranes dominating the skyline.

Captain Neven gazes out at it.

'All new. None of this building here in communistic times. All new. Italian money.'

He shakes his head. He remains resolutely unimpressed. 'In Croatia, nobody would let them to build such buildings. Not on the coast.'

But not totally pessimistic.

'I think they have good food, a bit like Turkey. Albania is eighty per cent Muslim country. We all have this five hundred years' influence of Turkey. In food and in mentality. In blood as well.'

'More so here than in Croatia?'

He nods and peers towards the shore.

'More here, yes.'

The radio crackles insistently. Someone is anxious to get in touch with us. Captain Neven ignores them. Three steep-prowed fishing boats cut across our bows heading out to sea.

The captain prevaricates until it's clear that the voices on the radio are ordering us to come into port and identify ourselves. It occurs to me as he reluctantly swings the wheel that, given his fatalistic suspicion of all things Albanian, Captain Neven thinks that once in he may never get out again.

We pull in past the sea wall to a compact, well-kept, not overcrowded port. There are two big ferry boats, in from Italy, only 70 miles away on the other side of the Strait of Otranto. Moored up against the long harbour wall are half a dozen battle-grey patrol vessels, apparently operated by the Italians, Albania's near-neighbours, and, since the demise of the isolationist dictator Enver Hoxha in 1985, once again their main trading partners.

At the dockside we're met by smartly dressed port officials who give our captain a dressing-down, in English, for not flying the Albanian national flag when in her waters. The captain, it transpires, doesn't have an Albanian national flag, but one is found for him.

We haven't been here long when a Mercedes pulls up beside the boat, and two thin men with short dark hair, swarthy complexions and unsmiling faces get out.

'We are press,' they announce with a certain flourish, fingering accreditation tags the size of breastplates. 'What do you think of our country?'

We reply that as none of us has yet set foot in it, it's hard to say.

They rapidly lose interest and are gone as swiftly as they arrived.

The next voice I hear in Albania has a broad Scots accent. It belongs to a short, sunburnt, hairy-legged man who, with a group of colleagues, is driving aid trucks from the Hebrides to Kosovo. He warns us that the roads are dire.

Eventually, all papers checked, we're allowed onto Albanian soil. Within minutes Captain Neven has turned around and is heading for dear life back to Croatia, the double-headed black eagle of Albania flapping from the rigging as he picks up the breeze.

**Below left**
*If it's Tuesday it must be Albania. Sunrise over the port of Durrës.*

**Below right**
*Hello sailors.*
*A welcoming committee at Durrës dockside.*

# Albania

**Day Twenty-three:** *Durrës*

Thunderclaps and the sound of rain lashing at the window punctuate an unsettled sleep.

The dawn view from the Hotel Adriatik is of a storm-ravaged sky, dark clouds massing on the western horizon, a pale sun fighting for survival.

The beach is lined with row after row of empty deckchairs.

Last night's meal here was pretty good, but breakfast is peculiarly depressing. Tinned fruit, slightly out-of-date butter and meagre strips of white bread in a dauntingly tall columned dining room with painted panels of Albanians in folk costume.

Among the few other guests are a couple, he Namibian, she Swedish, with a small child called Felipe. He's almost the same age as our first grandchild, Archie, born two months before we set out. Alert and quite devastating when he smiles, Felipe makes me suddenly and quite poignantly homesick.

Go for a walk along the shore. Unlike the rocky coast of Croatia, Durrës has a long and sandy beach, but it's hardly golden and already men are out working to clear the scum of marine matter swept in by last night's storm. Judging by the ranks of freshly built hotels and apartments Albanian tourism must be flourishing. Neon flashing signs reading 'Fast Food!' are everywhere. A lot of Kosovans come here for their holidays, I'm told.

At intervals along the beach is a chain of circular concrete bunkers ranging from 4 or 5 feet to 20 feet in height. Some lie half-collapsed in the breaking waves, others are sound enough to have been painted bright colours and turned into makeshift bars. There are 400,000 of these dotted all over Albania, which works out at one for every eight members of the population.

They are the legacy of Enver Hoxha (pronounced 'Hodger'), who led Albania into hardline Stalinist communism after the Second World War. When Stalin was discredited and the Soviet Union began to split with China over the future of communism, Hoxha took China's side, identifying with Chairman Mao's Cultural Revolution and declaring tiny Albania the first atheist state in Europe.

Paranoid about invasion, he not only ordered the construction of the bunkers, but made it illegal for Albanians to own maps of the country, and or to listen to the BBC World Service, a crime punishable by eight years in jail.

This had a cryogenic effect on Albania. Past and future didn't exist, and for forty years or so it was left in self-imposed isolation.

One effect of the rehabilitation of Albania since the hardliners left is that its history has been rediscovered, and found to be long and rich. A city called Epidamnus was founded here seven centuries before Christ. Changing its name to Dyrrachium, and later Durrës, it became one of the main supply ports for the Romans' eastern empire, and, interestingly, a hotbed of Venus worship.

There's little evidence of any hotbeds but Durrës does have the remains of Roman baths and an amphitheatre, which is the largest of its kind in the Balkans. It's not far up the hill from the harbour and though one side has had houses grafted

**Left**
*Looking like giant
jellyfish washed ashore,
a few of the 400,000
concrete bunkers put
up to guard Albania
during the Hoxha
regime dot the beach
at Durrës.*

onto it, enough is preserved to help the imagination fill the terraces with a 15,000 full house baying for blood. The tunnel from which the gladiators emerged is still there and my guidebook tells me that during excavation they unearthed forty skeletons with their necks broken.

Today the area around the floor of the amphitheatre is green and swampy and all that emerges from the tunnel is the sound of hundreds of frogs croaking.

Outside the amphitheatre is another layer of history, a city wall 6 feet thick and 25 feet high, built of brick and rubble with antique capitals embedded in it. It dates from roughly 1,500 years ago, when the Roman empire had split and this area was ruled from Constantinople. From this time onwards Albania was effectively a part of Eastern Europe and remains even now one of those countries least influenced by Western thought and ideas.

Then I met Ardi Pilaj. With his constantly demanding mobile, white trainers with red laces, black velvet jacket, ear studs, and Germany 2006 rubber wristband, he's no different from any young man on the streets of the West, and his attitudes are fresh and well informed, as befits a journalist working for, among others, the BBC.

He's accompanying us on the train to Tirana, and as we've time to spare we go for a coffee near the station. An apologetic waiter is about to serve us when the electrical supply cuts out. He suggests somewhere across the square but just as we get there their supply goes off as well. Ardi says the problem is not the availability of electricity, it's down to a distribution system that hasn't changed since Hoxha's time. Albania has not, like some, made a smooth transition from the days of communism. In 1996 their economy was shattered by the simultaneous collapse of a number of pyramid-selling schemes followed by near-anarchy in the streets.

A small group of children follows us from the café to the station, rubbing their stomachs and putting hands up to their mouths. They can't be more than ten or eleven, but they have the creased, prematurely aged faces of fifty-year-olds. Inside the station itself, a bare, functional slab of a place, people move slowly, dully. A world at half-speed.

**Right**
*The Durrës-Tirana train. Ardi Pilaj brings me up to speed on Albania.*

The sparrows, darting and wheeling above our heads, are the only creatures with any energy.

A Czech-built diesel locomotive brings in the train from Tirana and we climb aboard. Though most of the windows are cracked or shattered – children with stones, says Ardi – a team of lady sweepers moves methodically through, brushing up every speck of dust.

Tirana is no more than 25 miles from Durrës and the journey takes a little over an hour. The flat plain rises to low hills crowned with billboards on which the names of Albania's new friends are writ large. 'Vodafone', 'Heineken', 'DHL'.

Ardi talks about his country. He's weary about its image abroad, as a haven for criminals, sex-traffickers and the like.

'You haven't seen many criminals, have you?'

I smile and shake my head.

Ardi spreads his arms. 'I would feel safer in Tirana walking at night, than in Amsterdam or Paris or London, you know.'

For him the bigger problem is not criminal gangs but the exodus of skilled Albanians, the brain drain that has seen so many intellectuals and qualified people leaving to work abroad, in Greece, Italy and the United States. Until they come back Albania will always lag behind the rest of Europe.

We reach the outskirts of the capital. Homes are built right up against the line, and the train horn is in constant use. The old-fashioned houses, packed tight together with small gardens smothered in vines, could be in the countryside. Men play chess reclining on a grassy verge inches from the train.

In the Stygian gloom of Tirana Central the few passengers dismount. I watch an elderly man in a black suit shuffle slowly across the track to relieve himself by a fence, whilst his wife, equally smartly dressed and holding an umbrella, stands on the railway line and waits for him.

With its pervasive smell of rotting rubbish, and complete absence of any facilities whatsoever, Tirana Central is not a place to linger. Even the station approach is a

**Left**
*A smart lady waits for
her husband on the
platform at Tirana.*

gentle upward slope of mud, which we pick our way through with some care only to find ourselves, quite abruptly, in the middle of big city noise, light and bustle.

We walk the length of Zog One Boulevard, named after the king who led Albania into the Second World War, on Hitler's side, but spent most of it in a private suite at the Ritz in London. By the time we've reached the wide and rather grand space of Skanderbeg Square, in which every other car is a Mercedes, memories of Albania's dark, neglected railway are beginning to blur.

## Day Twenty-four: *Tirana to Krujë*

Skanderbeg (real name Gjergj Kastriot) is Albania's national hero. He won fame for rallying his country's resistance against the Ottoman Turks in the fifteenth century and in the square that bears his name he is commemorated by a handsomely fierce equestrian statue set atop a chunky stone plinth. The fact that all his courage and tenacity was ultimately wasted is gently rubbed in by the building next door to him, the small but perfectly formed mosque of Et'hem Bey, one of the Ottoman Turks who, after the death of Skanderbeg, ruled here for 434 years, until Albania was finally granted independence in 1913.

The rest of the square is a mixture of communist and fascist, from the wide triumphal boulevards built by Mussolini's architects in the 1930s, to the National Museum with a fine Social Realist mural above the entrance and the mighty columned Palace of Culture, currently home to a touring version of *Madam Butterfly* by Opera Macedonia.

Tirana appears much less dysfunctional than I'd expected. There are cafés where a cup of good espresso can set you back a *lek* or two and a street named after Lord Byron. (He spent time in Albania in the early 1800s meeting, among others, Ali Pasha, according to Robert Carver's book *The Accursed Mountains* 'an enthusiastic life-long pederast and paedophile' who boasted of personally killing 30,000 people.

Byron found him very charming, with a beautiful singing voice.)

What impresses me most is the way in which the post-war concrete housing blocks have been quite strikingly painted, not just in one colour but with a real artistic touch, mosaics of primary colours, chequerboards, diamonds, stripes and triangles picked out in washes of red, yellow and green. Little bays have been built onto the facades to break down the monotony of the outline.

The man most responsible for this grooming of Tirana is the socialist mayor, Edi (pronounced 'Eddie') Rama. Recognising that he can't afford to demolish all the dull and soulless housing of the communist era, he came up with a policy he has called art in building. In consultation with the occupants he has put a team of artists to work on decorating whole neighbourhoods.

In 2004 Rama was voted World Mayor of the Year.

A famously busy man, and an artist himself, he's agreed to meet me at his office, in one of the ochre and claret-painted Italianate terraces overlooking the southern end of Skanderbeg Square. We walk down corridors that are anything but institutional, painted with carefully chosen rich, dark colours and lined with quirky art.

Rama is in his forties I should think, grave, taciturn and very tall with a shaved head. He wears baggy black trousers and a big black collarless shirt with a fine red stripe. He looks like a man of the night. His eyes are dark and hooded and this world of crepuscular colours creates an ambience that is more Dracula's bedroom than council chamber.

His office is equally idiosyncratic. Irregular, almost diamond-shaped, it's painted a restful maroon with dark-red wood panelling. Scrolled out across the wall behind the long desk is a huge computerised enlargement of a photo of the city seventy years ago.

I take some comfort from a quick glance at his desk. A bowl of colouring pens sits next to a pile of business papers and his screensaver is a picture of himself and his young daughter.

As soon as we start talking about Tirana and his plans for the city he becomes a changed man, from monosyllabic to polysyllabic.

'It was a different city when I came in. It was basically without hope any more. After communism we passed from nightmarish collectivism to wild individualism, which was not democracy, it was more an anarchy. People built everywhere. Public space disappeared, physically and mentally.'

His administration began by demolishing 2,000 speculative buildings.

I ask him about the bowl of pens.

He gives a smile, bleak but encouraging.

'This is my box of medicines. Just to escape mentally from boring meetings.' He reaches for some sheets of paper which are covered with meticulous doodles.

'The minutes of last week's meeting?' I ask.

He nods. 'Yes. The therapeutic diary, you know.'

Boring meetings seem to have been his inspiration. From the colouring-in of these elaborate doodles came the idea for the painted buildings.

'Colours are part of our life and it's really a pity that cities are not reflecting this.' He gestures to the window.

'Tirana has a big potential…because we don't have a really strong tradition of

architecture, we don't have buildings of which we should be really proud...so the only way to keep them updated with the contemporary world is to colour them. If every building would be painted, every corner would be painted, it'll be amazing you know.'

For him this is not just an aesthetic thing. He calls it 'politics with colours'. A way of supporting democratic change at street level. I've never understood why cities have to be so grey and I'm rather fired by his enthusiasm.

'This is a first, isn't it?'

'Many things are. We were first in Albania for blowing up all the churches and the mosques and becoming the only country in the world without any religious practice. It was a very bitter first. I hope this can be a sweet first.'

We walk out together into Youth Park, an area where a mass of concrete has been cleared and replaced with fountains and cafés. Just across the river is 'The Block', a square mile or so which was once reserved for the villas of the communist elite and off-limits to ordinary Albanians. Hoxha's rather interesting modernist house remains, part of it now, by a supreme irony, given over to an English-language school.

Edi remembers the Hoxha years.

'The whole country had maybe 200 cars.... Private cars were not allowed, private life was totally controlled. Cafés didn't exist. We were isolated from West and East. It was like a concentration camp.'

He reaches out and shakes my hand.

'But, of course, freedom has also its own difficulties you know, so...'

He smiles, turns and with long, slow strides heads back through the trees towards his office. Two middle-aged women on a park bench rise in unison as he passes. An older man salutes him and they stop and talk. The charismatic Edi clearly has friends, but he also has powerful enemies, from the top of the national government downwards. His vision of Tirana as the world's first art city is a brave one, which would help put Albania back on the international stage and hasten the climb out of isolation and paranoia. But I fear that many of Edi's natural supporters are living abroad. He, more than anyone, needs to reverse the diaspora.

Tonight, just about ready for bed, when a cacophony of thumps, whooshes and screams splits the silence. Rush to the window expecting to see some gang shoot-out on the streets below. Instead I see a salvo of rockets and an arc of red, blue and silver

**Above left**
*Politics with colours. How to brighten a drab city without spending too much money.*

**Above right**
*Edi Rama, artist-mayor of Tirana, shows me his 'therapeutic diary'.*

starbursts rising high above the city. Where are they coming from? The gardens of the mayor's office. Where else?

## Day Twenty-five: *Krujë*

Today we get to see for ourselves the fabled pot-holes of Albania, for we're driving out of Tirana to the hill town of Krujë. After some mild rattling through the streets of Tirana, the really good vibrations begin about a mile from the hotel at a notorious interchange called the Blackbird Roundabout, so named after a brothel of the same name which used to stand on the site. It's an ambitious mess, more half-started than half-finished, caught in a deadlock between mayor and Prime minister. Whilst they argue, the roundabout resembles a slowly moving car park. A section of motorway, unconnected to anything else, lies stranded in the middle of this chaos, like some ancient dolmen.

Once past this stretch of urban no-man's-land things improve. A narrow highway lined with an unfeasibly large number of furniture warehouses, petrol stations and good old-fashioned ads with cowboys pulling hard on Marlboros takes us out along the flat plain to the north-west of Tirana.

This neither country nor city road is a touch depressing, and not helped by the appearance of the word 'Shitet', on many of the buildings, though this, I'm later assured, means 'For Rent.'

Krujë is dominated by a terrific battlemented castle set on a rocky crag with a fine view across the plain and out over a hazy Adriatic. In the same year as Henry V was inspiring English soldiers on the battlefield of Agincourt, the Turks swept into Albania and captured this mighty fortress. Enter national hero Skanderbeg (who had learnt his fighting from the Turks) to retake Krujë and hold it against

**Right**
*The Skanderbeg Museum at Krujë, built during the Hoxha years to extol the national hero who held off the Turks for many years. Turkey has not completely disappeared from the country, as you can see.*

not one but three Turkish sieges.

His success is the reason for all the bazaars, museums, guest houses, restaurants and lines of schoolchildren filling the cobbled streets and pathways. The defence of Krujë, though ultimately unsuccessful, is seen as the golden age of a country without a lot to celebrate. Krujë is a national shrine.

Illir Mati, my guide, is a cheerful, chatty, middle-aged Albanian, much given to smacking one hand with the palm of the other to reinforce his, many, opinions. His father was an admiral and he himself spent twenty years as a submarine engineer. When Albania was part of the Warsaw Pact they had twelve Soviet submarines but after Hoxha split with Russia this was reduced to four. Three of these were, as he put it, 'for show'. Only one was maintained, and that saw little action. Ordered to keep an eye on 'enemy activity', they patrolled the Otranto Channel and used their periscope to scan topless sunbathers on Italian beaches.

We walk up to the castle through a bazaar selling peasant furniture, wooden cradles, butter churns, cow bells, water jugs and Albanian flags and scarves. Vehicles aren't allowed up here so heavily laden donkeys push their way through. Illir pithily sums up Albania's transport revolution.

'From donkeys to Mercedes in twenty years. With nothing in between!'

Like everyone else I've asked, Illir seems unable to account for why, in a country of straitened circumstances, there should be so many Mercedes.

He shrugs, as though the answer's obvious. They're smuggled.

'People working very, very hard in the communist period, and all working for the State. Today, everyone work for himself. He don't believe in the work in Albania. Albania is a rich country, rich with oil, minerals like chrome, but what is main export now?'

'Tell me.'

'Prostitutation.'

**Left**
*High above Krujë, I walk with a pilgrim up to the Bektashi monastery.*

**Above left**

*The sheep is sacrificed to bring good fortune to the family working abroad.*

**Above right**

*The* baba, *the Bektashi holy man, lights up after doing the business.*

He counts off on his fingers.

'All we have to export now is prostitutation, drugs, weapons.'

In the castle I fall into conversation with a rather serious boy from a school group. They see very few foreign tourists and are interested in trying out their English.

'This is a beautiful country,' he says. 'But the government...'

He puckers up his nose.

'You know...'

'What don't you like about the government?'

'Well,' he says, and points to a corner of the castle. 'You see the tower there?'

'Yes.'

'It smells.'

'Ah.'

'They should keep it clean.'

We both nod and I move the conversation onto the safer ground of the World Cup, which begins in Germany today.

'Next time Albania will be there I hope.'

He smiles politely, but I have a sense that the smelly tower worries him more.

In the afternoon Illir and I scramble up the mountain to a monastery of the Bektashi religion, one of the offshoots of the Sufi order of Islam. Brought from Turkey by *babas* (fathers) or dervishes, it was never an institutional, organised religion, relying instead on personal communication with God through mystical folk beliefs, often close to paganism.

We are accompanying a young pilgrim from the village below who is taking a sheep to be sacrificed by the *baba*. His mother had a dream in which members of the family working abroad appeared to her and the sacrifice is the best way to stave off any harm the dream may have intimated.

After a slow climb through scrub and scree and dramatic limestone overhangs we reach the complex of buildings on the top of the mountain and are led into the presence of the *baba*. He is dressed in a thin white robe with a long green jacket over it and a multicoloured band around his waist. On his head is a green fez-like cap. He's clearly a prodigious smoker, his white beard stained almost mahogany around the mouth.

He sits, looking vaguely impatient, on a bed of cushions in front of a carpet with a large stag pictured on it. On the walls are framed pictures of holy men, the largest

**Above**
*Celebrations at the pilgrim's house. A daughter dances, a mother hands out home-made raki.*

of which depicts an illustrious convert to Bektashism, Pasha Tepelena, builder, statesman, friend of Lord Byron and one of the most enlightened of Albania's Ottoman rulers.

When we are all introduced and seated on our cushions an assistant, in clothes as drab as the *baba's* are bright, brings a succession of offerings. First, a bowl of wrapped boiled sweets, then, after an appropriate period of appreciation, a bowl of wrapped chocolates (which look suspiciously as if they've been gathered from the world's hotel pillows), followed by glasses of thick peach juice, cigarettes and, finally, glasses of *raki*. The *raki* and the cigarette seem to break up an awkward atmosphere, but what really cheers the *baba* up is when I make the awful gaffe of raising my left (unclean) hand to my heart during one of the toasts.

From here on we get on like a house on fire and he insists that I come down the steps with him to watch the sacrifice from close range. Try as I might I can't move further than 3 feet away, as the *baba*, surprisingly deftly, upends the sheep and swiftly draws the knife across its throat. Blood pumps out and the sheep writhes and shudders. With one of the last jerks of its back leg it catches the knife with which it's just been despatched, sending it spinning across the floor towards me. Then there is silence.

The pilgrim, immensely cheered by the sacrificial visit, invites us to have a drink and some food with him down in the village. He's one of four brothers of a handsome family whose business is coopering. Festivities take place beneath the cherry trees in a little garden outside a house his father has just bought. Bulbs dangle from exposed wires, tangles of pre-stressed rods poke out of the concrete and garlands of electric cabling hang down from the windows. An abundance of food and drink is brought round by the women and children whilst the brothers gather round to make music, the sheep-sacrificer on the mandolin, three others on clarinet, accordion and tambourine, and father on the fiddle, as they say. One of the granddaughters, in a fine white dress and an embroidered black waistcoat, dances a nimble variation on what could just as well have been a sword dance or a Highland reel or a sailor's hornpipe.

The light slowly fades, along with any Anglo-Albanian inhibitions. I can't think of a better way to spend the last night of my brief visit to this secretive country than up here in the hills in the back garden of someone I don't know, singing songs in a language I can't understand. Tonight, in our various ways, we're all celebrating. *Gezuar!*

# Macedonia

### Day Twenty-seven: *Ohrid*

The plodding Balkan highway, the E852, that enters Macedonia from the Albanian frontier, was once the illustrious Via Egnatia, a hugely important trade route, carrying goods from Italy to Constantinople. It was laid down by the Romans to join their empire with another they'd just conquered, the empire of Alexander the Great. Or as he's remembered here in his homeland, Alexander III of Macedon.

Today there's nothing left of the Via Egnatia or the trade that once must have flowed along it. The E852 connects the poorest country in Europe with the poorest country of the former Yugoslavia. Yet there is something about this first view of Macedonia that has power and presence, that makes you feel that whatever has befallen the country is a temporary aberration. This is a corner of Europe where history is made, not merely suffered.

It's all to do with the charismatic presence of Lake Ohrid. Overlooked in the west by the steep frowning mountains of Albania and by broad forested slopes to the east, it demands respect. Measuring almost 20 miles long and 10 wide, it plunges to a depth just short of 1,000 feet.

There has been a lake here for at least three million years, making it one of the oldest in the world, comparable with Titicaca and Baikal. It's perhaps no surprise that there are believed to be 350 religious establishments around its shores.

Tonight its waters are dark and agitated, sending explosive walls of water bursting against the promenade. Clouds of spray fly over the 'You Are Here' tourist map which, a little sad and damp now, helpfully points out not just the local churches but also where to go for body piercing. On a plinth nearby the sculpted figures of the tenth-century saints Clement and Naum stare out at the troubled waters. They are credited with inventing the Slavic language and Clement, a disciple of Saint Cyril, is thought to have devised a new alphabet, called Cyrillic, which is still in use across Russia as well as here in Macedonia. It's a sign that we're moving away from Central European influences and into the Slav Orthodox countries and the Russian sphere of influence.

There are few people about and the only two who come over to talk to us turn out to be Serbians who complain that the Macedonians won't change their currency. We help out by exchanging euros for the Serbian dinars which they're almost inexpressibly grateful to get rid of.

We find a waterfront restaurant called Dalga in the cobbled Old Town which serves the famous Lake Ohrid trout, but in portions as big as the lake itself, and this after an abundant *ordever* (hors d'oeuvres) of red peppers, feta, Parmesan cheese, salami and Croatian prosciutto. The walls are covered with photographs of the patron with various high-profile visitors. Mostly in black and white and degraded by time and the weather, they look as if they're all out of FBI files.

Filled to the brim with food and good Macedonian wine, we run the gauntlet of crashing waves along the promenade, coat collars tucked up.

## Day Twenty-eight: *Ohrid*

**Above**
*Wild skies above Lake Ohrid, one of the oldest, deepest, most revered lakes in the world.*

Slight feeling of déjà-vu this morning when I discover that our hotel is located on Quay Marshal Tito. The great man clearly had a thing about lakes for he had a palatial summer home here, to match the one at Bled in Slovenia, Ohrid and Bled virtually marking the eastern and western limits of his Yugoslavia.

For good measure, there's a formidable fortress overlooking the lake here too. Its sandy-brown walls girdle nearly 2 miles of hilltop. It was built by Samoil, a Bulgarian who, after his armies wrested his country away from Byzantine control, was crowned king of Macedonia with Ohrid as his capital and borders that stretched over most of the Balkans. It proved to be one of the world's least resilient empires, lasting a mere twenty years before the armies of Byzantium won their land back. After their defeat in battle, Samoil's army was systematically blinded on the orders of the Emperor Vasilius, leaving one eye for every hundred men, to enable them to find their way back home.

I meet up with Kaliopi Bukle, an Ohrid-born singing star of the former Yugoslavia now married to an elfin-slim, and much younger, actor called Vasil.

She's sensible and down-to-earth as big stars go, mid-thirties, attractive in a homely sort of way, but concerned enough about her looks to have a make-up artist in tow. When I ask her if there are things she misses about Yugoslavia, her brow furrows in concentration then clears almost instantly.

'Smells!'

She doesn't immediately elaborate so I'm left wondering if this is literally what she misses or some kind of metaphor.

'I'm missing the smell of the old time in Yugoslavia. When I think about the

things I love in my life, everything has his smell.'

She laughs rather sweetly and apologises for her English. (Why should she? I know only one word of Macedonian: *zdravo*, hello.) When she goes on she's thankfully off the smells and onto more pragmatic ground.

'It was a different thing singing for twenty million people then, and two million people today.'

This is the same nostalgic refrain I'd heard from Lado in Slovenia and the Croatian captain on the boat from Dubrovnik to Durrës. And I don't think it was just about making money, but more an assertion that whatever might have been wrong with Yugoslavia, it was artistically and culturally a better place then than now.

We walk around the *Mesokastro*, the Old Town, beginning at a gnarled and stooped old plane tree which has supposedly been hanging in there for 900 years. They know it as the Cinar tree and it's the symbol of the city of Ohrid. Up the hill, past a few well-restored old houses with storeys attractively cantilevered out one above the other, is the amphitheatre, not as big as the one in Durrës, but impressive enough to show how important Ohrid was to the Romans. Once we've done very old things there isn't a lot to see. Modern Ohrid is undistinguished and scarcely does justice to the beauty of its situation.

We end up at a taverna by the waterfront.

My eye is drawn irresistibly to the lake. It's magnetically attractive, especially today when fast-scudding clouds and wind-rumpled water combine to create a shimmering, constantly changing play of light and shade.

I ask how they get on with their neighbours across the water. Vasil says they have good relations with the Albanians, though there are issues about dumping waste in the famously pristine waters of the lake.

Other neighbours are more problematical. After the break-up of Yugoslavia the Greeks insisted that if Macedonia were to be given independence it should be called the Former Yugoslav Republic of Macedonia (Fyrm), to distinguish it from the Macedonian region of northern Greece. It was only in 2003 that, for the first time since the end of the Second World War, the Greek government issued visas for Macedonians to visit relatives on the Greek side.

There's even been a long-running dispute over ownership of Alexander the Great, who was born in what is now Greece, but spoke Macedonian.

Kaliopi spreads her hands, helplessly.

**Above and opposite**
*Life on the streets
of Ohrid, ancient
town and centre of
Macedonian tourism.*

'I don't understand what is "Fyrm", it's nothing to me.'

But the Greeks take it very seriously. Vasil was at a recent arts festival in the Ukraine from which the Greek contingent walked out after the organisers referred to him as being from the Republic of Macedonia.

Kaliopi's love for her country seems unequivocal, like their love for her. She struggles to find the words to best express the relationship.

'I am like paprika for the Macedonian people!' she declares, which takes me a bit by surprise.

'Paprika?'

She nods eagerly.

'Because the Macedonian cannot live without paprika, and maybe that is the best compliment for me.'

Paprika or otherwise, it's significant that when she goes on to talk about the many new projects she has with Vasil the one that enthuses her most is a musical of the life of Marshal Tito.

Macedonian she may be on her passport, but Yugoslavia still exerts a powerful spell.

## Day Twenty-nine: *Ohrid to Prilep*

East from Ohrid the road swoops up and over a landscape of high passes and thickly forested slopes which broadens into a wider rolling plain. A town appears, dominated by weirdly eroded rocks, the white scar of a marble quarry and a monumental, derelict fortress built by King Marko, a Serbian who became Macedonia's last king before the Ottoman invasions.

This is Prilep, a modest town, currently in the throes of a beer festival and preparing itself for tomorrow's Festival of Saint Mary, or as she translates rather spectacularly in Macedonian, Saint Bogorodica. The centrepiece of the religious celebrations is not in the town itself but in a monastery 6 miles away, tucked so snugly into the smoothed and sculpted rocks that you have to get right up close before you believe in it.

There is a dirt road, but on holy days ninety per cent of the worshippers take the old cobbled path and a two-hour walk from the road below.

We're met at the fine, frescoed gatehouse of Treskavec monastery by the only

monk in residence here, Brother Kalist, a tall, straight-backed, gentle man in a black robe, circular black velvet cap and with a long, curly beard streaked with grey. Once an economist in Macedonia's capital Skopje, he's now training for the priesthood.

The grounds of the monastery are already filling up with people who will spend the night here before tomorrow's festival, but Brother Kalist, despite being continually buttonholed about this and that, takes time to show us around.

There have been establishments of various kinds up here in the shelter of the mountain since pre-Roman times. Recent archaeological work has uncovered remains of a temple to Apollo and fragments of sculpted toga-wearing figures can be seen, incorporated into much later walls.

The compact basilica at the centre of the monastery has a pair of elaborately patterned doors, each one carved from a single piece of wood and depicting not only scenes of the life of Christ, but also a Buddha. They're supreme examples of the work of the Prilep School of Flat Wood Carving, Brother Kalist tells me proudly. In the narthex, where people are lighting votive candles, there are paintings from the fourteenth century and the decorations in the main body of the church are fifteenth century but look distinctly modern in their treatment of flowers and animals.

Brother Kalist points upwards. 'Have you seen our Gaudí ceiling?'

I peer up obligingly. It's a moment before I notice the twinkle in his eye.

'I tell my Spanish visitors it's by Gaudí.' He looks rather pleased with himself. 'Just for a joke.'

My favourite building in the complex is the sternly functional 650-year-old vaulted refectory, with its table made from one long stone block with niches cut around the base into which the monks could fit their feet. A long, finely carved gully runs down the centre along which bones and other left-overs could be sluiced away.

Brother Kalist regrets that he will have to leave us now, as the mayor of Prilep has arrived for the evening mass. I have the feeling that his visit is a rare event, less to do with devotion and more with appearances.

## Day Thirty: *Prilep*

Sunrise on Saint Bogorodica's day and I'm being hauled slowly and noisily up the damp clay track to the monastery in a thirty-five-year-old, ex-Yugoslav army, Fiat jeep.

'Alfa Romeo engine!' shouts my driver above the screaming roar, as he revs us round another steep and slippery bend.

I'm put to shame by the column of people already making their way up on foot: old, young, male and female, families with children, many carrying gifts and money for the monastery.

We also pass quite a few groups of spiky-haired teenagers. In England you'd be pushed to find them out of bed at this time, let alone walking to church.

When we reach the top and are welcomed once again by the ever-attentive Brother Kalist, I ask him

**Opposite**
*In the Treskavec monastery above Prilep, with Brother Kalist. Behind us is the fourteenth-century Church of St Bogorodica. People walk miles to worship here.*

**Below**
*Driving up the mountain to the monastery in my Alfa Romeo-powered jeep.*

**Right**
*St Bogorodica's day at
Treskavec monastery.
The bishop offers the
bread he's just blessed.*

about them. He tells me they always have a lot of students at this particular festival day, as it's just before the schools and colleges go back and they're here to get the Virgin Mary's blessing for the next school year. He gestures approvingly at the groups already staking out their places on the grass, even though the sun's barely risen.

'We are a young church.'

It points to the remarkable resurgence of religion in Macedonia after the Tito years when priests were not allowed to practise. Brother Kalist won't be drawn on politics, but he speaks with great admiration of the people of Prilep who made sure their monastery was kept open and looked after during those difficult times. I suggest to him that the church may appear to be above politics but it's surely a much sought-after political ally.

He concedes the point. 'Oh yes. That was why the mayor was here last night.'

A middle-aged man appears up the last steep slope of the path. He's clearly run up the hill and his T-shirt is sodden with sweat. He stops, rocking on his legs, takes huge gulps of air, crosses himself at the threshold of the monastery and walks respectfully inside. He's followed by groups of young men, sprinting then sauntering up the hill and pausing to hurl schoolyard abuse at their friends below. But no matter how laddish they are, they too cross themselves before entering the monastery complex, and three times if they're going inside the church.

After a two-hour morning mass has been sung, specially prepared bread and cake is set out on a platform in the grounds. Preceded by a black-robed nun swinging a censer, the prodigiously bearded and pony-tailed bishop, in an embroidered cope and bejewelled mitre, blesses the food, water and wine. He's accompanied by three young men who sing lovely, mellow chants. Afterwards they tell me, with some pride, that these are recently rediscovered eighth- and ninth-century Byzantine Macedonian works.

Another symptom of resurgent Balkan nationalism you might think, but these

**Left**
*A boy lights a votive candle in the church. Many of the worshippers are young people, asking for God's blessing at the start of a new school year.*

singers are not little Macedonians. They speak excellent English, are huge fans of Pink Floyd and very excited at the visit of the Pet Shop Boys to Skopje in two weeks' time.

Today's celebrations are by no means solemn. This is as much a community as a religious event and the meal that is now served up is prepared and paid for by a local family. I'm invited to sit at the top table with the bishop, the deacon and 'Kalist', as they all call him. A homely atmosphere as fathers, mothers, uncles, aunts and lots of children wait on some 250 of us at a single long table.

We're served a thick bean soup, with coleslaw salad, cold fried fish, freshly blessed bread and sweet cake. The bishop offers me red wine, made in the monastery. A huge glass is poured, Kalist looking on rather apologetically. 'Not quite up to standard yet,' he mutters, and he's right.

Next to me is a burly tank of a man, who's the head of a construction company which has done a lot of work in the rebuilding of the monastery and he and his family will be next year's sponsors. He's an Alexander the Great fan, and talks of his frustration at the richness of the archaeology in Macedonia and the difficulty in raising money to preserve it.

Treskavec is packed tight as the time comes for us to leave and yet in a couple of months it will be the start of winter. St Mary's Day will have come and gone, the children will be hard at work and the only occupant of this mountain-top eyrie will be Brother Kalist. I wish him luck and ask him when he will become a fully qualified monk.

He looks bashful. 'It's not up to me. The bishop is deciding that.'

'I'm sure you're wishing he'll make up his mind soon.'

'The monks don't have wishes,' he smiles and looks around him and out over the great sweeping plain beyond. 'But if I had some wish, my wish would be to die here in the mountains.'

It's a three-hour drive to the Bulgarian border, through lakeland scenery, green meadows and wooded steep hills. The human scenery is less attractive. Towns are small, run-down and dominated by shoddy apartment blocks. I have the feeling, admittedly on very short acquaintance, that Macedonia may have suffered most from the break-up of the Yugoslav Federation. Within Yugoslavia it had the strength and support to survive. Without, it is fragile and vulnerable. Average earnings, I'm told, are around 250 euros a month. Their security depends on old Russian fighters and Bulgarian tanks and Mafia influence is widespread. Even their national flag, an eye-catching gold-on-red rising sun, which we see for the last time fluttering above the border post beyond Delčevo, had to be changed after complaints from the Greeks that it incorporated the star of Vergina, the symbol of the ancient Macedonian kingdom to which the Greeks lay sole claim.

Unlike comfortable Croatia or even ignored Albania, Macedonia is a country trying to convince the world that it should be taken seriously.

We walk up the hill into Bulgaria. The first, and indeed only building beyond customs and immigration doesn't look promising. It bears the faded name 'Snek Bar', and it looks as if it closed down years ago. Then I notice signs of life. A donkey is grazing in the long grass beside it and from within I hear a dog bark. A man with a wild look in his eyes and an axe over his shoulder appears from nowhere and heads inside. I follow him, a little cautiously, thinking a cup of coffee might not go amiss. A fetid smell, a combination of bad food and unwashed dogs, makes me move smartly away, but not before I catch a nightmarish glimpse of an old woman, and a dog, dressed up like a child, sitting in a chair.

# Bulgaria

**Day Thirty-one:** *The Rila Mountains*

I'm woken at half past five this morning, but I didn't need to be. I've been mentally marking off the minutes for almost an hour. It may be summer in the Balkans but in my tent, beneath clear skies and on a mountainside 7,500 feet up, the cold comes as an unwelcome shock.

There are some thousand people camped around me and I'm already worrying about how we're all going to fit into five toilets. Struggle to dress and clamber out of the tent. And there are all my neighbours of the night, huddled beside calor gas lamps or heading down the hill by torchlight towards what's laughingly called the bathroom block. It was dark when we arrived here yesterday evening, by four-wheel drive along the near-vertical course of a dried-up stream and then by horseback, so I've little idea of quite where we are. All I know is that it's a place special enough to be chosen for the annual coming-together of the White Brotherhood, a non-drinking, non-smoking community of vegetarians who follow the teachings of one Peter Deunov, whom they call The Master, and on whom the Spirit of God descended on 7 March 1897.

I try to find out a little more but it isn't easy. A tall, long-haired rangy figure in the tent next to me is a doctor, who gives off the irritating air of someone who

knows more than I ever will, however hard I try.

Are you all members of the Brotherhood, I ask. He reproves me quite sharply. Of course not. They're not members of anything. More tentatively I ask if their choice of this place is an expression of their religion. Wrong again. They are not a religion.

'Our Master said,' and here he fixes me with ominously clear eyes, 'with paneurythmy I give you a weapon, it is for you to use it right.'

There is no time for me to ask what the hell paneurythmy is as everyone is getting up and heading up the mountain to greet the sunrise.

Sartorially, the White Brotherhood is a bit of a let-down. Most of my fellow sun-greeters are in anoraks and windcheaters of every shade but white. We congregate on the edge of a rocky bluff. Hundreds of us clinging to whatever foothold we can find. As J-P, our director, observes, it's like a human puffin sanctuary.

Unlike in the tents last night, there is almost total silence. A reverent hush. Light slowly fills the sky to reveal a dramatic landscape. Directly below us a rocky slope falls away to a lake. Beyond that a panorama of interlocking mountain spurs stretches as far as the eye can see. A thin mist rises as if the whole land has been freshly baked.

Looking up at the faces around me I'm reminded of the Easter Island statues. Grave and passionless faces all turned to the horizon. Then, slowly, right hands are raised, palms open, directed at the new light. When the sun is fully risen the hands are lowered and for the first time there are sounds from the multitude: prayers, low chants, people reading from texts, some thin music.

I'm as glad to see the sun as they are, and my mood is transformed as it illuminates the full glory of the place they call Sedemte Ezera, Seven Lakes, the spectacular heart of the Rila Mountains.

At breakfast I'm introduced to a young man of regular good looks, wearing sandals, white linen trousers and a sensible sweater who could be, and it turns out is, an IT programmer on his day off. His name is Dimitar and I gather he is quite high

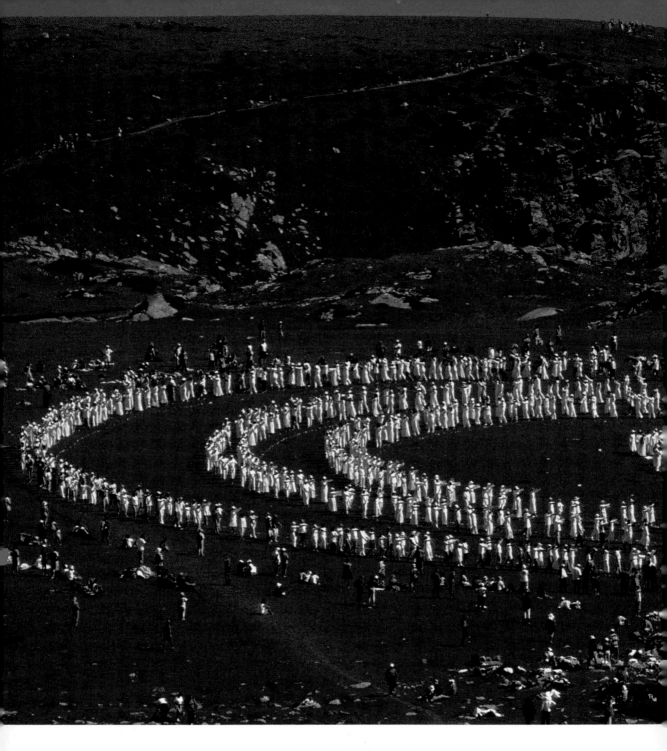

up in the hierarchy of the White Brotherhood – if indeed they have a hierarchy, which they don't.

Perhaps he can at least tell me what paneurythmy means.

'It's a spiritual dance.'

'Ah.'

I ask him why the Brotherhood should come to dance in such an inaccessible place.

'It's because of the spiritual nature of the energies here.'

It turns out that The Master, Peter Deunov, an impressive figure who, in photos, looks like a cross between Abraham Lincoln and Rasputin, was the one who first

identified the Seven Lakes as having special qualities.

'High energy, high vibrations,' Dimitar explains.

I'm quite relieved when, in mid-morning, the campers set out, en masse, for the upper slopes for the aforementioned paneurythmic dancing. The theory may be nebulous but the practice promises to be quite spectacular.

I'm not disappointed. Climbing a steeply winding mountain path up from the campsite, I emerge onto a broad saddle of grassland and there ahead of me, framed by grey rock walls, dabbed with patches of unmelted snow, over a thousand people dressed in white are moving slowly round in huge concentric circles.

It looks less like dancing and more like one of those mass PT displays the Chinese

**Above**
*Mass paneurythmic dancing, the highlight of the year for the White Brotherhood.*

are so fond of. Breathing deeply and regularly, and emitting a low cosmic hum, the participants raise and lower their arms (in what I'm later told are variations of the thirty-seven movements laid down by The Master), point their bare feet at an angle to the ground and stare beatifically off into the middle distance.

After half an hour or so there's a welcome change of tempo, from the near-funereal to the almost jaunty. The choreography becomes gradually more ambitious. Circles stop and face the centre, turn and move the opposite way, break up and reform in a series of kaleidoscopic patterns, and all in near-silence.

Gone are the anoraks and fleeces of the sunrise ceremony. The all-white dress code has been largely observed and with the sun, the mountains and the clear glacial lakes all being in the right place at the right time, the White Brotherhood and their paneurythmic dancing make an inspiring sight.

This being a national park, and a weekend, curious spectators appear. Walkers dressed in shell-suits or shorts that look like underpants stop and stare, or blast away with their cameras before waddling on and I find myself admiring the Brotherhood for their poise and stillness and, yes, style.

When it's all over I join Dimitar and his family for a picnic. They're good people, bright and generous with their time. But as Dimitar explains once again about love, harmony, circles, symbols and the prayer of movement and dance I realise that they are the converted. Their Master's voice has a relevance for them that cannot easily be shared with outsiders. They're more interested in protecting their purity than selling a watered-down version to the rest of the world. As we begin our long descent from this beautiful place I reflect, a little wistfully, that perhaps the White Brotherhood is not the place for a meat-eating, wine-loving comedian.


## Day Thirty-two: *Godech*

Stefan Kitov, known to all as 'Kita', works in the film business in Sofia, and is a great fan of *Monty Python*, but an even bigger fan of *rakiya*, the powerful local brandy which has seen Bulgarians through many troubled times. He is most concerned that I should not pass through his country without tasting the real thing, as made by his father.

So it is that I find myself, an hour's drive from the capital, passing through deserted swathes of agricultural land on my way to the small town of Godech.

Kita confirms that Bulgarians are not only moving off the land but their birthrate is falling too. With a national population the same size as London this is not good news, but Bulgaria has never had a lot to celebrate. One of the many tribes emanating from Central Asia, the Bulgars were first noted by the Emperor Constantine as 'a race of new and vulgar people' from the north Balkans. Even when they did get their act together, as they did under King Samoil in the tenth century, they were quickly slapped down by the army-blinding Byzantine Emperor Vasilius (later immortalised for bloodthirsty schoolboys as Basil the Bulgar Slayer).

Following the fall of Constantinople, Byzantine occupation gave way to Turkish, and another 400 years passed until, in the Treaty of San Stefano of 1878, Bulgaria became independent again.

**Left**
*In the Bulgarian
countryside, Kita
(left of frame) discusses
the finer points of
home-brewed* rakiya
*with the two producers,
his father and me.*

A series of self-inflicted blows followed, and after ending up on the losing side in two world wars Bulgaria survived, like Hungary, as a classic example of a small country that had been much bigger.

Unlike Tito's Yugoslavia, which did comfortably well by playing off East against West, Bulgaria threw in its lot firmly with Stalin and the Soviets. In the 1980s it alienated its substantial Turkish minority with an extreme policy which required them all to change their names into Bulgarian.

Only recently, with accession to NATO in 2004, did the course of history begin to turn to their advantage and the possibility of EU membership in 2007 would seal a triumphant turnaround.

Kita shrugs off the vagaries of their history. What can you expect, he says, of a people who nod for no and shake their heads for yes.

'We always do things the other way round.'

In Godech, on the gentle slopes of a broad valley, police have pulled over a motor-cyclist, whilst a man walks past them on the pavement, leading his cow. Kita's father bought a plot here thirty years ago and built his attractive little house himself. He was deputy director of a sports goods business.

'Deputy director was the highest he could get without joining the Party,' Kita explains wryly.

A house like this, modelled on the Russian dacha, served an important purpose for people at that time, not just as a place to grow one's own food but as a political safety valve, an escape from the rules, restrictions and supervision of the socialist State.

'Socialism was a system of limits,' says Kita. 'On a plot like this you could set your own limits.'

His father, a straight-backed, sharp-eyed, restless man, takes me on a tour of the garden, showing off tomatoes, peppers, cauliflower, spring onions, cucumber and pumpkins of considerable girth, all grown, he is at pains to point out, without the

**Above**

*Tzeta sits outside the still with a huge bottle of* rakiya. *The cat waits for more sausage.*

aid of any chemicals. He also shows off his rabbits, an outdoor shower made from old bits of sheet metal, and his new extension.

But it's the trees he's most proud of. Apple, pear, wild plum. There's only one rule. He won't plant a tree that can't produce *rakiya*. In vain does his wife suggest a nice walnut or a decorative maple. If it doesn't bear fruit, he's not interested. Which is the cue for us to follow this indefatigable old man down to the house of two equally old and indefatigable neighbours, Lubo and Tzeta, in whose back garden the best *rakiya* in Bulgaria is made. So they say.

It's in many ways an idyllic place, a repository of unreformed village life, with a donkey grazing at one end and coal-black chickens at the other. The donkey is completely placid until the camera turns to film my entrance, whereupon it becomes almost frantically active, rolling on its back and emitting a salvo of well aimed farts.

Beneath an apple tree, a table has been set with glasses, bottles of water and a plate of grilled sausage, already being attended to by a cat which darts out from behind an upturned wheelbarrow when it thinks you're not looking.

Lubo and Tzeta, solid and silver-haired seventy-year-olds, show me the shed in which they've been distilling *rakiya* for the past twenty years. The fruit mix is heated by a wood fire and rises into a copper still called the *kazan*, before cooling down and running out, rather prosaically, into a brown plastic bucket. The process is then repeated to strengthen the alcohol content. Tzeta dips a thermometer into a cracked glass test tube and pronounces that what's in the bucket today is fifty-two per cent proof.

When I ask how long they leave it to mature there's general laughter. Laying it down is a luxury. Or as Lubo puts it: 'There's no bad *rakiya*, only little *rakiya*.'

I ask if bootleg *rakiya* like this will be outlawed if Bulgaria joins the EU.

Kita nods a little gloomily. 'You know it's the same with the size of the cucumber. When we go to the European Union they'll want us to make exactly the same size of cucumber and they will want to stop this sort of breweries. But,' he warns, 'I think there will be a real revolution in Bulgaria!'

The meal that follows is a triumph of unbureaucratic self-sufficiency. Starting, in the traditional Bulgarian way, with *rakiya*, both of plum and prune, we have peppers in batter, aubergines stuffed with cheese, a plate of Bulgarian white and yellow cheeses, a red wine called No Man's Land, and, to finish off, cold beers.

As we all join the cat in tucking into the *meze* Kita raises a glass for two toasts. The first is to his favourite film. 'When I saw The *Life of Brian* the first time I fell twice from a chair.'

The other toast is to the donkey.

## Day Thirty-three: *Sofia*

I'm in the garden café of a smart hotel in the intimate, walkable centre of Sofia. A quartet of soberly but elegantly dressed conservatoire girls are tuning their violins and cellos. As they raise their bows and I raise my cappuccino, I take quiet satisfaction in having discovered this little oasis of civilisation.

So lulled am I by the pleasantness of it all that it's almost half a minute before I realise they're playing 'Tulips from Amsterdam'.

I leave with the strains of 'My Way' fading behind me and wander through the City Garden past a group of elderly and oddly disputatious chess players and an accordionist leaning up against a tree, counting the coins in an upturned cap. At the far end of the park are some gardens, laid out a few years ago on the site of what was once one of the most venerated places in Sofia, the mausoleum of Georgi Dimitrov, the father of Bulgarian communism, and Prime Minister from 1946 to 1949. By all accounts he was a very nasty piece of work who attended to the bourgeoisie with a pragmatic brutality that Stalin might have envied. On his orders thousands were killed or sent to forced labour camps, robbing his country of a generation of talent.

In 1990, following the abrupt collapse of the Soviet empire, his remains were removed, but the mausoleum proved so solidly built that it was not successfully demolished for another ten years.

Dimitrov and his friends have left their mark on the city. The wide plaza called the Largo was laid out by the communists after the Allied bombers destroyed much of central Sofia at the end of the Second World War. It's still dominated by the Party Headquarters building, but tucked in amongst the monumental stucco facades is a less boastful architectural gem, the Buyuk Djami, a mosque built in 1496. It now houses an archaeological museum. I've

**Below**
*Keep music live! The delightful musicians at Sofia's Grand Hotel playing their way.*

never been easily seduced by such places but this is a revelation. The collection is of incomparable quality, for Bulgaria sits on one of the greatest resources of ancient artefacts in the world. Even before the Greeks and Romans were here, and a thousand years ahead of the Bulgars, the land was home to Thracian tribes, rich enough to produce exquisitely detailed work in gold and silver and precious stones. Much of this was produced for the elaborate graves of the rich and powerful, who would be buried with their treasure all around them, to accompany their souls into immortality.

Their tombs are scattered across Bulgaria, many still sealed. What has already been unearthed is often extraordinary work, as graceful and intricate as anything that might be designed nowadays. For me the highlight of this dazzling collection was a Thracian gold-leaf death mask, made some two and a half thousand years ago. Powerful and delicately fine at the same time.

More modern workmanship can be found at the flea-market outside the exuberant explosion of domes and towers that is the Alexander Nevski church, which was built as a memorial to the 200,000 Russians who died fighting the Turks in the cause of pan-Slavism in the 1870s. Here, amongst stalls full of Nazi and Soviet memorabilia, I find whole regiments of Russian dolls painted to suit all tastes. Yasser Arafat, Saddam Hussein, Osama Bin Laden and George Bush stand shoulder to shoulder with the Queen, Tony Blair and Stalin. It was a toss-up, but in the end I did my patriotic duty and bought the Queen.

Sofia is not a spectacular city. The Bulgarians don't seem to do excess. Many of the city centre streets are narrow and tree-lined, more like those of a laid-back provincial capital. Few official cars race through, there is little triumphalism, and men in suits and ties are rare enough to be noticeable. The clothes look neither downtrodden nor particularly chic, the shops are up-to-date but lack flair, the people content but not demonstrative.

Which is why I'm rather looking forward to meeting a man described in my *Rough Guide* as 'Bulgaria's most controversial gender-bending phenomenon'.

Asiz is portrayed by some as the devil incarnate, by others as a very naughty boy but when we meet, in the modest, slightly shabby suite of rooms that passes for his office, I find myself shaking hands with a plump young man with peroxide blond hair and the shrewd smile of a wary attention-seeker. His skin is dark and a swirl of tattoos runs across his neck and shoulders and down beneath a black T-shirt. Not quite a choirboy, but very different from the huge posters of him on the wall in crutch-hugging glitter and full make-up. He's a delight to talk to, not just because he's nice and droll but because he so clearly relishes being different. He's Gypsy, one of an estimated 380,000 in a country of seven and a half million people, and he's gay, with plans to marry a man later in the year and adopt children 'from all over the world'.

None of which should endear him to the Bulgarian people, who seem quite old-fashioned in these matters. What makes it all work is the success of the *chalga* (Romany) music he performs so powerfully and the attraction of the flashy, loud, nouveau-riche lifestyle that goes with it. And he does love his mother.

When he was still a child she had what he calls 'sick ambitions' for him to be a mega-star like Elizabeth Taylor, but because he was Gypsy all the doors were closed. When I ask him who his audience is he says the underground world, prostitutes and gays.

'The free people,' he adds.

'And the Gypsies. Could there be others, inspired by his example?'

He shrugs his wide shoulders.

'They're still as dirty and miserable as they were. It'll never change.'

He's stubborn and patient and these are not Gypsy values.

'The problem with them is that they want something and on the next day something completely different.'

We talk about what it was like growing up in socialist Bulgaria. Did he have to join organisations like the Young Pioneers?

He grins less warily now. Yes, he was a Young Pioneer, but always wanted to wear the girl's uniform.

'I wanted to be the majorette rather than the football player!'

So what of the future?

Though he says he's a patriot and whenever he hears a Bulgarian song he's moved to shed a tear, he feels the country is now too small for him. Once his wild and raunchy transsexual persona shocked people here. Now they're only shocked when they see him in normal clothes. So he's contemplating leaving home to find fame and fortune elsewhere.

In America perhaps?

He shakes his head firmly. In America, he says, they'd probably throw stones at him. No, he'd like to work in London where, he reckons, you're free to do what you want and be who you want.

**Opposite**
*This is Orthodox country and icons abound in the streets near the Alexander Nevski Church in Sofia.*

A bodyguard moves position at the door and I realise that this candid and engaging man is also a big star and we've outrun our allotted time. Patient to the end, he finds time to pose for a few snaps beside the rudest poster we can find.

### Day Thirty-five: *Plovdiv*

Moving deeper now into the south-east corner of Europe, along the fast four-lane autoroute that connects Sofia and Bulgaria's second city, Plovdiv, across the Plain of Thrace. The landscape of heathland and low bare hills is undistinguished, and remarkably empty. In Western Europe a major highway like this would be a development magnet, studded with warehouses, distribution centres and business parks.

The present and the future may look a little subdued but the past is thriving in Bulgaria. Plovdiv is one of the oldest cities in Europe, first settled by the Thracians 7,000 years ago, then rebuilt in the fourth century BC by Alexander the Great's father Philip of Macedon, who modestly renamed it Philippopolis.

The Maritsa valley, in which the city lies, was a natural conduit for trade through the Balkans and the commercial importance of Plovdiv/Philippopolis is marked, as in Durrës in Albania, and Ohrid in Macedonia, by the remains of a large Roman amphitheatre, set on a hill with a perilously balanced wall of columns and pediments creating a dramatic frame for the city beyond.

I meet up here with Mira Staleva, a young woman born and brought up in Plovdiv. Record temperatures, above 40° Celsius, are expected later today and already the white marble terracing of the outdoor theatre is like a hot iron, so Mira and I take refuge at a café nearby. A mindless drum and bass sample thuds out, hugely

over-amplified. No-one is listening, but no-one seems to want to turn it off.

Plovdiv, says Mira, was a good place to grow up. It was a cultured city, tolerant and laid-back. 'It's very Mediterranean. I mean when you go for a coffee you go for at least two hours.'

There were Jewish, Romanian, Greek, Turkish and Gypsy quarters, and the only bad time she can remember was the ill-fated name-changing policy of the 1980s when those of the minorities who refused to change their name to a Bulgarian equivalent were victimised, being refused work and all benefits. She had many Turkish friends in school who were forced, temporarily, out of the country.

'I was sixteen or seventeen years old, but nobody reacted. It was really sad. The communist system can make you really passive, you know.'

Like Asiz, Mira was a Young Pioneer, and she remembers learning how to strip down Kalashnikovs whilst still at school.

'You go in the classroom with thirty Kalashnikovs on the desk and everybody starts. We check the time. It was like a competition, who would be first.'

'Who was the enemy?'

'It was an abstract enemy. But in the Pioneers' organisation you were "always ready".'

At sixteen she was attending military camp, wearing uniform and getting up at five in the morning.

'But it was the best time of my life, actually. When someone is trying to press you to do something, you find different ways to escape.'

Close by the Roman theatre is a network of cobbled streets, often huddled against remains of the old Byzantine city walls. Built along these steep slopes are houses as strikingly attractive as any I've seen on the journey so far. They date from the late eighteenth and early nineteenth centuries, and were built by merchants who had made money from trade with the Ottoman empire. With solid stone-walled bases and half-timbered upper storeys cantilevered out over the street, they also have distinctive wooden balconies, oriel windows, decorative plasterwork and louvred shutters. They create a sort of Alpine-Turkish feel and could well be the backdrop to those Orientalist paintings that nineteenth-century travellers to the Balkans were producing for an increasingly fascinated audience back home.

**Opposite**
*With Mira at one of the best-preserved Roman amphitheatres in south-east Europe, overlooking the city of Plovdiv, or Philippopolis, as it was named after Alexander the Great's father.*

One of those responsible for awakening this interest in all things Ottoman was the French poet Lamartine and his house, now open to the public, is one of the grandest in this picturesque little enclave.

Many of these houses were commandeered by the State after World War Two, but since the demise of communism a restitution policy has been under way and many of the original owners, or their families, have been given back their properties and are sympathetically restoring them.

Looking back at the city from the shallow, sandy river you can glimpse the hill where the amphitheatre stands, through a forest of eight-storey blocks made of prefabricated concrete. They are now mainly occupied by Gypsy families (also called Roma, or *Tsigani* in Bulgarian). Originating in India, the Gypsies made their way into Eastern Europe some 600 years ago, but have never really integrated with the local people. They're seen as outsiders who reject the social system, whilst enjoying its financial benefits. Mira doesn't see much hope. There are foundations and welfare groups who are trying to build a bridge between Gypsies and the rest of society but she can't see how it will work. Current figures bear out her pessimism. Around eighty-five per cent of Gypsies in Bulgaria are unemployed and only ten per cent of children are in secondary school education.

Today, with the help of the city council, we're trying to do our bit for Plovdiv's Gypsy community by providing pin money for a horse and cart racing event. A dozen contestants have come forward, some behind old nags shackled to rickety wooden carts, others perched on stripped-down frames of steel on rubber wheels. The race-track is a section of dual carriageway which has been blocked off for the afternoon.

The organisers, Gypsies themselves, are taking it very seriously. Pieces of paper are waved about. Children, half-naked in the heat of the day, crowd around us, curious, but not aggressive.

But there is aggression elsewhere. There seem to be two kinds of vehicle in this community, the horse and cart and the souped-up, flashily customised old banger, always driven to deliver maximum tyre squeal. It's one of these that threatens to completely ruin the first race. Packed with cheering and yelling punters, it drives so close to the lead horse that no-one can overtake it. This results in a protest of such ferocity that the protagonists have to be held apart. Exactly the same thing happens with the next race. The horses, besides being whipped to flared-nostril frenzy, have to put up with the squealing roar of a car and its occupants right beside their heads.

Eventually a winner is chosen and we're invited to join a party in amongst the blocks themselves.

The buildings are stained and the paintwork blistered and peeling. Uncollected rubbish is piled up, and stagnant puddles of sewage overflow the gutters. Between the blocks the occupants are sitting around in groups with waste, blown by the wind, drifting around them. Silhouetted against the strong evening sun they look like survivors of some apocalyptic disaster.

The party is getting under way in a yard between the blocks. A loud and brassy band is playing, massively amplified of course, and the floor is taken by a dozen or

**Right**
*Horse and cart racing in Plovdiv's Gypsy community. The supporters' cars terrify the lean horses.*

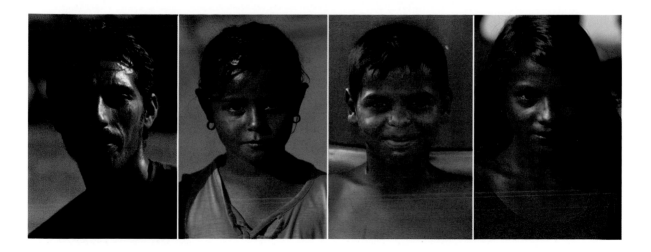

so elderly Gypsy women who gyrate rather gently to the cacophonous music. One of them has a gun, which she waves about her as she dances, occasionally taking aim at someone and grinning broadly. No-one seems to bat an eyelid.

**Above**

*Faces in the crowd. The Gypsies of Plovdiv.*

The menfolk look on, unimpressed, rolling up their T-shirts to reveal large and rounded bellies which they stroke from time to time as if they were much loved family pets.

Even our friendly organisers don't encourage us to stay on too long. Once darkness falls and the drink takes hold they can't ensure our safety.

For the moment I'm content to be the only man on the floor, with the undivided attention of a swaying harem of Gypsy matrons, some of them armed.

## Day Thirty-six: *Perperikon to Zlatograd*

As one does on a Monday morning, I find myself riding a mule up a steep track between oak, ash and hazel woods that leads to an 8,000 year-old city which an archaeologist (on horseback, ahead of me) thinks could be on a par with Troy or Mycenae.

The fact that I'm on a mule and he's on a horse says much about the Quixote-like character of Nikolai Ovcharov, the man who, by sheer force of his own conviction, has persuaded the Bulgarian government to spend good money putting the lost city of Perperek on the map.

Below us, bulldozers, excavators and graders are clearing and levelling a wide swathe of hillside for an approach road. Generators hum beside the new visitor centre. Minibuses from the surrounding villages are delivering some of the 130-strong workforce, and a line of gleaming new toilets stands amid the dust. This is archaeology as big business. And archaeologist as celebrity.

Nikolai Ovcharov clearly loves the attention. Well built, with a carefully trimmed grey-flecked beard, he has a strong, commanding voice and a touch of a swagger. Some call him the Bulgarian Indiana Jones, and with his safari hat clipped up at the sides and a knife sheathed on his belt, he seems quite happy to invite the comparison.

At the top of the hill my reluctant mule delivers me into a shady glade where a

**Above**

*Nikolai Ovcharov,*
*the Indiana Jones*
*of Bulgarian*
*archaeology, rests*
*in the saddle before we*
*head up the mountain.*
*My mule was reluctant*
*to head anywhere.*

couple of hammocks are slung and a rough table with wooden bench seats is set beneath a makeshift canopy of leaves. Smoke rises from a fire. This is command headquarters for the dig, but we don't linger as Nikolai strides off to inspect progress.

We're in the Eastern Rhodopi Mountains, in the land of classical legends, two hours south of Plovdiv and just 21 miles from the Greek border. Orpheus, the man whose music could charm wild beasts and make rocks and trees move, is said to have been buried here after being torn to death by women on his return from the underworld, and Spartacus raised his army against the Romans here.

The side of the hill is ringed with massive white rock faces, so spectacularly sculpted by the combined effects of rain, sun and earthquakes that it's hard to tell what is naturally shaped and what is humanly carved. Nikolai has no doubt that he has stumbled upon evidence of what he calls 'the culture of the Rock People', and points out a huge throne, holes in the rock where timbers were secured, fortified gates to the citadel, a stone-walled grid for fifteen graves, and a slab on which the marks of an ancient fire circle can be seen and where sacrifices would have been made.

For two months of the year a small army of students from Sofia University join local Bulgarian-Turkish labourers in Ovcharov's kingdom, mapping the site, marking the rocks, digging trenches and generally strengthening the case for Perperek as not only a sanctuary, fortress and sometime acropolis, but also one of the great religious sites of antiquity.

Whatever they find, Ovcharov's work is already done. By convincing himself and the Bulgarian government that it is everything he says it is, he has transformed a lifeless local economy, given tourists a more urgent reason to visit the beautiful

Rhodopi Mountains and made an international name for himself. Though to be honest, Napoleon suits him better than Indiana Jones.

Within a few months Bulgaria will be given some of the most momentous news in its recent history, when a decision on their European Union application is made. From what I see down here they have decided it'll go their way and that the border crossings into nearby Greece will be reopened. Considerable amounts have been spent upgrading the roads and local amenities (with signs not just in Cyrillic but in the Latin alphabet as well). A town with the unpromising name of Zlatograd turns out to have a wonderful collection of 200-year-old Bulgarian-Alpine houses, restored and brought to life in an Ethnographic Museum. The houses have pantiled roofs, tall white chimneys and deep wooden balconies on one of which we're treated to a last intense shot of Bulgarian cuisine. After a week and a half of the ever-present *salata shopska*, a mound of salad shrouded in grated cheese, these local delicacies are a revelation. Fragrantly spiced meat stew, cabbage leaves stuffed with rice yet light as a feather and a spicy bean soup called *bob*.

Afterwards we're served dense Turkish coffee, made in little copper pots and heated in the sand whilst three singers and musicians treat us to unique local music. The songs are delivered in a style I've heard nowhere else, a deep, resonant throaty flow of great, if controlled, power. They're accompanied by the equally unfamiliar strains of the *gaida*, a sheepskin bagpipe, with three tubes, one to keep the bag inflated, another to play the melody and a third the drone. On paper it reads like a formula for the most difficult way to produce a sound, yet they manage to make these old songs of love and longing intensely poignant. They tell me that an example of this remarkable way of singing is aboard the Voyager 2 spacecraft.

Which is as it should be. After all, Orpheus, the greatest musician of them all, was a local Rhodopi boy.

**Left**
*The temple at Perperikon, where Ovcharov thinks a powerful Oracle was worshipped 8,000 years ago. In the background the Rhodopi Mountains and the forests where the Orpheus legend was born.*

# *Turkey*

**Day Thirty-seven:** *Plovdiv to Edirne*

There is nothing very beautiful about the E80 interchange east of Plovdiv, but there is an excellent truckers' café, the Motel Merita, with an engagingly ebullient patron, fine kofta kebabs, succulent meat rolls and an irresistible speciality of metre-long loaves of bread, crisped in the oven and sprinkled with sesame seeds.

I manage to cadge a lift in the direction of Turkey with a big, full-bellied man with a remarkable head. Almost exactly pyramidal in shape, it tapers from a bull-like neck to a small square crown. He hauls himself up into the cab and surprises me by getting out a very neat pair of horn-rimmed glasses, as if we were in a library instead of a 40-foot truck.

He's a friendly man and his few words of English are mostly destinations. I learn that one of his recent journeys took him all the way to Uzbekistan. Two weeks there and back doing 430 miles a day.

We pull out of the parking lot, a sudden halt to let another vehicle pass sending a row of hanging icons swinging above the windscreen.

After a mile or two we come to a sign that sets the pulses racing. Well, mine anyway. 'Istanbul'. Two hundred and eighty-five miles down the road.

Late afternoon. Crossing into Turkey at a village called Kapikule. The Greek, Bulgarian and Turkish borders all meet here as Europe funnels down towards Asia. A large mosque is marooned in no-man's-land, but apart from that there's nothing remotely attractive about this place. Blighted by the frontier, Kapikule seems to consist of little more than a lot of concrete tarmac, a lot of steel fencing, a huge gantry with the badge of Turkish customs at its centre, a filling station, a railway line, a truck park and ploughed fields, strewn with paper bags, stretching away on either side.

I take a taxi the few miles into the nearby city of Edirne. Flanking the four-lane autoroute are a scattering of functional buildings, small hotels and modest houses flying big red flags bearing the star and crescent moon of Turkey, an oddly Islamic symbol for a secular republic with no official religion.

Going the other way, a long line of trucks moves slowly westward. Whatever the outcome of their government's bid to join the European Union, Turkey's businessmen seem to be there already.

A first and quite thrilling glimpse of the skyline of Edirne, dominated by the massive domes and soaring minarets of one of the finest mosques in the world.

Closer up the city is less dramatic. The streets are busy, the lights are coming on and shoppers are out in force. There are supermarkets in the main street and in the side streets people sell fruit and vegetables off the back of pick-up trucks. Our hotel is tucked away amongst a cluster of low buildings of varying ages and states of repair. Inside it's like a small museum. Big, comfortable, old-fashioned armchairs and sofas are surrounded by all sorts of period bric-a-brac. Adding machines, sewing machines, an old steam iron, a reel-to-reel tape recorder, a trumpet. It's a time-capsule of the 1930s.

An open fire rounds off the distinct impression of not being in Turkey at all, but a thousand miles away. In England.

## Day Thirty-eight: *Edirne*

My bedroom at the idiosyncratic Hotel Efe continues the cosy, but culturally confusing, Agatha Christie theme with some bakelite fittings, dodgy wiring and lovely old glass lampshades. I leave it early, and rather reluctantly, to explore the city with Selen Korkut, our translator, whose family comes from this most westerly part of Turkey.

We're drawn first, and quite naturally, to the crowning glory of the city, the Selimiye Cami mosque, designed by Mimar Sinan when he was in his eighties. It is considered to be the finest work of the finest architect the Ottoman empire ever produced.

Built like a small mountain range, it has eighteen subsidiary domes clustering around a single spectacular cupola with the whole complex marked at each corner by graceful sandstone minarets, which at 232 feet are the tallest outside Mecca.

There is a chain low across the arched gate of the mosque, designed to make sure that one enters with bowed head, but once inside the central prayer hall our heads go up again, in sheer wonder at the immense scale of the place. Eight sturdy supporting columns raise a dome 103 feet across and 144 feet high, with no central support at all. The genius of the architect is to make this colossal weight of stone look light and airy, hovering above us as if suspended from the heavens, rather than raised above the earth. It's by no means an exclusively Islamic statement. In shape and style it owes much to the great Byzantine church of Aya Sofya in Istanbul, built

**Right**

*Dazzled in Edirne.
With Selen in the
Selimiye Cami mosque,
masterpiece of the
great Ottoman
architect Sinan, who's
buried in the grounds.*

almost ten centuries earlier, and though the Ottomans came originally from Anatolia in the east, Sinan was a military architect who had travelled all over Europe and must have seen Renaissance masterpieces like Brunelleschi's dome in Florence.

Nevertheless prayer here, with two thousand others around you, must be a powerful experience for a Muslim worshipper. I ask Selen, very much a modern Turkish woman, if she goes regularly to the mosque. She shakes her head. Prayers can only be spoken in Arabic, never in any other language, so if she wants to pray she would have to learn the Koran. And there was me assuming, stupidly, that Arabic and Turkish were somehow the same thing.

The reason the city is so richly endowed with fine buildings is that for forty-five years before the fall of Constantinople, Edirne was the capital of the Ottoman empire.

It has three other great Ottoman mosques, down the hill and less dominant than the Selimiye Cami. Eski Cami, the Old Mosque, is square in shape with nine domes, and on one of its outer walls the words 'Allah' and 'Mohammed' are spelled out in giant calligraphics. It was built between 1403 and 1414 as the Islamic armies of Sultan Mehmet II were beginning to encircle Constantinople, slowly squeezing the life out of the Christian empire that had lasted there for over a thousand years. Across the road is the Üç Şerefeli Cami, the Mosque of Three Balconies, whose minarets are all different. One is plain fluted, and the others all decorated with red sandstone patterns, one in chevrons, another in diamonds, and one with red spirals, like a maypole, a marvellously fluent feat of masonry.

The architectural treasures of Edirne exude the confidence of conquerors.

Selen takes me a little way out of the city to see one of her favourite buildings, a multi-domed mosque complex of austere beauty apparently stranded amongst ploughed fields.

The Beyazit Kulesi, built in 1485, just over thirty years after Constantinople finally fell to the Ottoman Turks, was intended by its founder to be much more than a mosque. It was also a school, guest house, mill, bakery, public bath, soup kitchen, and most intriguingly of all, a psychiatric hospital, which has been restored and opened as a Health Museum.

Entering a walled enclosure, we pass a row of domed consulting rooms giving onto a small garden and sheltered by an arcade. At the end of this two arches lead into the *darüş-şifa*, the healing house, where for nearly four hundred years those with mental illness could be treated with the most enlightened methods like music, odours and the sound of flowing water.

Each room has life-size figures illustrating various aspects of the therapy.

In one there is a melancholic, someone suffering from what Selen calls 'black love' or what we might call a broken heart. Another is labelled 'Room for Treatment by Keeping Busy', what we might call 'occupational therapy'.

The *darüş-şifa*, supported entirely by charitable donations, is all the more remarkable when you think that right up to the nineteenth century the only place for the insane throughout most of Europe was the madhouse.

Ironically the asylum here, having operated under the Turks for almost four centuries, closed its doors in 1878 when the Russians occupied the area and the Congress of Berlin confirmed the beginning of the end of the Ottoman empire.

As surprising to me as the existence of a four-hundred-year-old psychiatric

**Above**

*Olive oil wrestling. After competitors have oiled themselves, the pairs of wrestlers stand in traditional pose; right; as the* cazgir *announces them with a poem and a quip.*

hospital is the news that Selen, a small, serious, Istanbul liberal, went out for two years with a man who made a living from wrestling, while covered from head to foot in olive oil.

Not only that but she's taking me down to the banks of the River Meriç, which forms the border between Greece and Turkey, to watch this bizarre sport in action.

'Why oil wrestling?', I ask her.

Selen smiles. 'Turkish men are very macho,' she explains, 'and they have to do something about it. When my father was young he was always with oil wrestlers. Even before he went to school he was pouring for them.'

'Pouring?'

'You'll see.'

What I see as we arrive at a woodland glade beside the river is a number of bulbous men wearing only tight, black, buffalo-skin pantaloons (called *kisbet*), being doused in diluted olive oil which they rub all over their bodies, with no particular sense of urgency, as if they were in a shower. Two of the wrestlers are young boys, no more than eleven or twelve I would think, who look like cheerful ragamuffins from an *Oliver* chorus line. Selen says it's common for the up-and-coming to learn alongside their elders.

On the back of their pants is a name, which Selen tells me is that of their sponsor. This may be a small warm-up event, but these men are all professionals, and at the big summer festival their fights can be watched by thousands of people.

'It's a very traditional Turkish sport,' Selen assures me. 'It has 640 years of history.'

Whilst the wrestlers (known as *pehlivani*) oil themselves up, a band of musicians, another vital ingredient in the sport, are also gathering. They wear loose blue waistcoats and baggy trousers with black-embroidered patterns and their instruments consist mainly of drums, *davul*, and oboes, *zurna*.

At last an announcer, the *cazgir*, brings them all together. Before the bouts begin, and some of them can last up to ninety minutes each, the *cazgir* introduces the competitors in his own inimitable fashion, often with a poem or a few jokes.

'The crowd love these people,' whispers Selen.

When the grappling eventually begins, all the pairs fight at the same time, supervised by a referee for each of them. Victory is achieved only when you can get your opponent flat on his back. Punching is not allowed, nor poking in the eye, but other-

94

wise the rules of contact seem quite liberal. As it's almost impossible to get a grip on the lavishly oiled bodies they are allowed, nay encouraged, to slip a hand down the trousers of their opponent and use the buttocks as leverage, whilst the other hand grabs at the leather hem of the trouser just below the knee.

Intense concentration is required, and very often two slippery men will just lean upon one another, breathing in great heaves and waiting, sometimes for several minutes, for the moment to surprise their opponents. The band plays its part too, dictating the tempo of a bout by slowing down or speeding up the rhythm.

There is no danger of the physical effort becoming any easier once the oil is rubbed off, for attendants are prowling with fresh supplies and reanointing glistening bodies whenever possible. Now I know what 'pouring' is all about.

At the end of each bout, victor and vanquished have to hoist each other off the ground in a manly hug.

It sounds absurd, grown men covered in olive oil, hands down each others' trousers, but there is a curious dignity to the whole procedure. Nothing is arbitrary, moves are carefully worked out and sanctified by a history and tradition that goes right back to the Greeks and Romans. But it has been refined into something wholly Turkish, something that strikes a deep and patriotic chord in the country people.

## Day Thirty-nine: *Istanbul*

The train from Edirne pulls into Sirkeci Station. Not the largest station in Istanbul but the most famous, linked for ever with the Orient Express, the train that, in various shapes and forms, has connected Turkey with the rest of Europe since 1883.

**Left**
*Wrestlers in action.
Buttocks can be used
for leverage.*

**Above**

*On the Galata Bridge, which crosses the Golden Horn. The poster, sponsored by Istanbul City Council, bears the words of Kemal Atatürk, founder of modern Turkey: 'Our most sacred duty is to keep the Republic alive'.*

It's a delightful small station with an original roof supported by three graceful rows of cast-iron columns that follow the curve of the platform.

Our Zagreb-built locomotive squeals to a halt, face to face with the man who created modern Turkey, Kemal Atatürk, whose gold-painted head protrudes from a stone plinth beside the buffers. With his long straight nose and beetle-browed stare he looks vaguely sinister, like a magician. Which, in a sense, he was.

In little more than ten years he created the Turkish Republic, separated religion and state, introduced the Latin alphabet, and gave women full voting rights. It's particularly appropriate that his likeness should be here at Sirkeci for he did more than anyone to turn Turkey's mindset westward, towards Europe.

I leave the station, down a flight of marble steps and into Istanbul. The city doesn't work its magic straightaway. There's a filling station and some ugly concrete blocks to negotiate before you reach the waterfront. And there you are, quite suddenly, at one of the crossroads of the world.

Nowhere do history and geography merge as spectacularly as they do here, at the end of Europe and the beginning of Asia, where the Mediterranean meets the Black Sea. The great north–south, east–west corridors meet here and the city built on these low hills, by its various names of Byzantium, Constantinople and Istanbul, has been at the centre of world affairs longer than any other.

The location seems to heighten ordinary experience. Views seem more dramatic, departures and arrivals more significant, encounters more promising, awareness sharper. Istanbul always strikes me as a city with a foot in two distinct worlds and I can't imagine it ever jumping completely onto one side or the other.

As Orhan Pamuk says in his book on the city, 'Istanbul's greatest virtue is its people's ability to see the city through both Western and Eastern eyes.'

I set out across the Galata Bridge, my back to the great Ottoman and Byzantine monuments, heading up to Pera, once a colony of Genoese merchants. Fishermen line the bridge and flat-topped water taxis slide beneath it with inches to spare. On the piers are huge posters quoting Atatürk, 'Our most sacred duty is to keep the Republic alive'. These strident reiterations of republican ideals suggest that people need reminding of them, which in turn suggests that they're under threat.

Opposite Galatasaray School, at a fashionable, very westernized café named after him, I meet Ara Güler, one of the most experienced documentary photographers in the world. He looks and sounds wise, with a big strong grizzled head, bald at the top and heavily bearded at the bottom. He is still digesting the news that has rocked the country of the assassination, two days ago, of the Armenian Hrant Dink, a liberal writer and publisher. Güler knew him well, had played poker with him a few days before.

'I took rather a lot of money off him,' he says, with a rueful grin, as if he was saying what his friend would have expected him to say in the circumstances.

The news coming through is that his killer was a young man from Trabzon, on the Black Sea, an extreme nationalist who regarded people like Dink and Nobel Prize-winning author Orhan Pamuk as bringing the country into disrepute by, among other things, daring to mention Turkish genocide of the Armenians ninety years earlier. Before dismissing the assassin as a madman, it's worth remembering that this same attitude is enshrined in law here. Article 301 of the Turkish Penal

**Left**
*Breakfast with Ara Güler, the internationally renowned photographer, so famous they named this place after him, Kafe Ara.*

Code makes 'denigrating Turkishness' an offence.

Ara, a Jew and also an Armenian, is shocked but not altogether surprised. He lived through the trauma of a few years ago when four bombs went off near here, two one day, two the next, aimed at synagogues and British interests in the city. Two years before that sixty-four people were killed when a local synagogue was bombed.

There are threats to the Republic from both sides, from religious extremists and nationalists, and though the authorities are anxious to appear on top of the situation it is having an effect. Visitor numbers from Europe were down by eleven per cent last year though they're now climbing again. But Ara Güler, for all his fame and his international connections, has Istanbul in his blood and would never consider moving. He's just got himself a digital camera and he sets off to show me his favourite part of the city.

'Every day I discover a new Istanbul,' he tells me as we clamber up some steep steps in the Jewish quarter where once fine old buildings now seem old and neglected, unsteady and unloved, leaning on each other for support. He takes pictures of these old neighbourhoods because he fears that much of what he loves about the city will soon be gone for ever.

'We are walking in the dead body of Istanbul,' he declares, adding, 'the smiling dead body.'

'Smiling?' I query.

'No, no! Smelling. The smelling dead body.'

His friend Orhan Pamuk has said that Ara Güler's photographs show an Istanbul 'where there is as much melancholy in the faces of the city's people as in its views'.

Pamuk seems to think that melancholy is the prevailing mood of the city, a mood he clearly approves of, and which he feels is in danger of being threatened by money and materialism. Istanbul has certainly boomed since I was last here on my way from *Pole to Pole* in 1991, with two new bridges over the Bosphorus and a number of dull but unavoidable modern towers muscling in on a skyline that was once dominated by domes and minarets.

To avoid becoming too much affected by others' regrets, I take a ferry into Asia, and up into one of the many suburbs spreading out over the exposed hillsides of the eastern bank of the Bosphorus. This is new Istanbul, without decay but without character, where everything is fresh out of the box.

**Below**

*The modern face of belly-dancing. Tanyeli goes through some moves for pupils at her Academy, also known as Tanyeli's Dance Clinic.*

**Left**
*Why can't men
belly-dance? Tanyeli
puts her finger on the
problem.*

In one of these security-gated suburban villas I find Tanyeli's Dance Academy, where people can learn to belly-dance like Turkey's greatest star.

Tanyeli is the go-ahead, hard-working face of Turkey's enterprise culture. Not content with being able to move her belly in almost any direction, at any speed, she has built herself into a brand, with a television show and a chain of similar academies as far afield as Florida and Australia. She's bright, sublimely confident, in very good shape and effortlessly in control of the three girls she's teaching today. At the end of a session with them she has a brief pit-stop when make-up checks her hair, wardrobe checks her clothes and as she takes a call on her mobile, someone else towels down her armpits.

When I ask her when she started to belly-dance, she spreads her arms wide, 'I think it started in my mother's tummy.'

She certainly knows how to sell it to a modern audience.

'It is like a meditation. If you feel the music, and if you know how to move your belly, you lose your negative energies and you don't have to run to the pharmacy to get your little pills.'

I ask her if she can teach belly-dancing to men.

She grimaces.

'It doesn't belong to men. The belly-dancing history started thousands of years ago when a woman wants to give birth and all the girls tell her to push it, breathe in, breathe out. So do you think it belongs to you or it belongs to us?'

Nevertheless she politely inspects my tummy and asks me to roll it for her. The best I can do is a rather obscene pelvic thrust.

'Think about salsa, samba, waltz,' she says sweetly, but firmly. 'Any kind of dance but not belly-dance.'

**Below**

*Ancient and modern
on the Bosphorus.
A 1990s suspension
bridge carries traffic
between Europe and
Asia, and the Rumeli
Castle was the Ottoman
army's bridgehead
when they captured
Constantinople in
1453, and changed its
name to Istanbul.*

## Day Forty: *Istanbul*

A boat up along the European shore of the Bosphorus. Meeting Ara Güler and reading Pamuk's *Istanbul* have sharpened my senses and I search the coast for signs of the fast-disappearing *yalis*, the elaborately stylish timber houses built as waterfront retreats for the city's prominent families. Few have survived the weather and the insatiable appetite for property by the water, and those that survive remind me of the houseboats in Kashmir, delicately beautiful, made for pleasure not for permanence. What they do show is how Ottoman architects and craftsmen of the nineteenth century were absorbing more and more European influence. It worked both ways and the French, as Lamartine's house in Plovdiv showed, were particularly fascinated by things Oriental. (Pamuk punctures any rosy picture of this relationship by pointing out that the nineteenth-century euphemism for syphilis in Turkey was *frengi* or 'French'.)

We pass the well preserved ruin of Rumeli Castle, whose walls ride up the hill, almost immediately below a suspension bridge that carries six lanes of cross-Turkey traffic across the Bosphorus. Rumeli, ominously for the Byzantines, was the Ottoman word for 'west', and, completed by Mehmet II in 1452, it was the springboard for his conquest of Constantinople a year later. A victory of the East over the West, Islam over Christianity.

The new conquerors of Istanbul are still to be found beside the Bosphorus and one of them is Sakip Sabanci, once a cotton-picker from the southern city of Adana, now a self-made businessman of such wealth that some say he owns Turkey. He has spent a

**Above left**
*Only a boat trip on the
Bosphorus gives you a
real sense of Istanbul's
stunning location.*

**Above right**
*With Raffi Portakal
and the Sabanci family,
some of Turkey's richest
benefactors.*

fortune turning a 1920s villa in Emirgan into a home for his fine art collection.

Here I meet Raffi Portakal, a debonair art dealer who has advised on the collection. He is bemused by the idea of Turkey not being thought a part of Europe. Even leaving aside the 500-year Ottoman presence in Eastern Europe, Constantinople was, for 1,000 years before that, the eastern outpost of Rome. Christianity survived here when Rome was being sacked.

As evidence for his country's continued interest in things Western he tells me of the Picasso exhibition he recently put on. Though entry had to be rationed to 2,000 a day, a quarter of a million people visited. This was not just the Istanbul elite, but people from all over Turkey. Indeed the exhibition will soon be going east to the capital, Ankara. For Raffi, the equation is quite simple.

'The Turkish people like the Western art, because the Turkish people are Western.' Which is why he is so frustrated about European behaviour over his country's membership of the EU. 'We know as a club member you have to accept many rules, but if the club start to create different rules... ' His words are obscured by a crowd of schoolchildren, all in neat private school uniforms, who emerge in a babble from the museum.

The thorny question of whether women in Turkey should wear the veil is addressed in an highly original way by Rabia Yalçin, who designs haute couture for Muslim women from an apartment five floors above the busy streets of Nişantaşi. Since the Republic was set up in 1923, Turkey has prided itself on separating state and religion and, like the French, does not permit women to wear the veil on state premises.

Rabia Yalçin, a small, doughty lady with a great sense of humour, wears a headscarf as she shows me her sensational, defiantly sexy outfits for Muslim women who want to maintain respectability without losing their femininity. Two tall, impassive models from Belarus demonstrate the dresses, one of which plunges down to the hip at the back, but can be easily covered with a whisper-thin veil.

This compromise between religious belief and feminine beauty is a very modern view, and one which I dare say traditionalists, especially men, would have problems with. Does it shock people, I ask her.

'Oh yes,' she says with a flashing smile. 'I like shocks.'

I'm in for another surprise in the evening as we visit one of Istanbul's old taverns, known as *meyhanes*. They are unpretentious neighbourhood places serving an uncomplicated fare of *meze*, *raki* and live music. The oldest *meyhani* in town is the Madame Despina Meyhanesi, which has been in business for 160 years. Its big bear of an owner welcomes us to what he says is 'the oldest entertainment culture in Turkey', beloved of artists, intellectuals and craftsmen. I read somewhere that they were all-male establishments, but that doesn't seem to be the case tonight, and I fall into conversation with a voluble Turkish woman who warns me against jumping to easy conclusions about her country. Istanbul is not all of Turkey, she says, and what Istanbul thinks is not the same as what the sixty million in the rest of the country think.

As far as membership of a wider Europe goes, she believes the question is not how much the EU needs Turkey, but how much Turkey needs the EU. Her agricultural system would almost certainly not survive the European competition.

She urges me to go east and see what people think there.

I'm halfway through a plateful of kidney beans, ratatouille, red peppers, beetroot and a glass of the aniseed-flavoured *raki* when an attractive woman with long earrings and dark hair pulled back introduces herself and sits down beside me. My hopes rise briefly, only to be dashed by the arrival of the house band, a daunting quartet of violin, drums, screechy oboe and a magnificent multi-stringed zither, which clusters around her as she serenades me with a heartstring-tugging number.

She's called Sevval, she sings in ten languages, and has an English boyfriend called Rupert whom she met on a beach. Her songs are part of an old tradition of classical Turkish music peculiar to the *meyhani*.

'Turkish people really love to be sad, you know. The songs make an imitation sadness.' The name *meyhani* is, says Sevval, a combination of two Turkish words, *mey* meaning drink and *hani* meaning house.

'And you start to drink *raki* and listen to this kind of music and you start to open your heart and cure your soul.'

'Rather than wine or beer?'

'Oh yes,' she assures me, 'because with this drink, you are going to wake up better tomorrow.'

With this Holy Grail of all drinkers in mind, I have my glass filled and wait to have my heart unlocked, and my soul cured.

**Opposite**

*Barbecues and balloons as the Selçuk crowd settles in for a day's camel wrestling.*

## Day Forty-one: *Selçuk*

At the entrance to a natural amphitheatre formed in the lee of a hill beside the deep blue Aegean Sea there hangs the splendid sign, '25th Selçuk-Ephesus Camel-Wrestling Festival'. The names alone are epic, Selçuk being the home of the first Turkic tribe to test the Byzantine hegemony and Ephesus once designated capital of Asia by the Romans.

It's a fine day with clear skies and smoke is drifting from barbecues already cooking sausages and kebabs for the expected 20,000 camel-wrestling fans.

On the curving slope hundreds, if not thousands, of white plastic chairs and tables are laid out and on top of the hill is a steel frame to which has been lashed a huge likeness of Atatürk, looking dapper, as he always did, in an astrakhan hat.

The fact that this event is set out in the open, rather than in a specially built stadium, makes it a very folksy, traditional affair, part county fair, part point-to-point. This is essentially a country sport, a celebration of the camel and all it represents in Turkish culture – the nomadic life and the camel trains that brought goods and prosperity along the Silk Road. No matter that there are hardly any working camels left in Turkey, no matter that those who will be wrestling here today are the pampered pets of those that can afford to keep them, no matter they're more like racehorses than beasts of burden, there is something reassuring about the camels. Something that inspires deep affection. Camels are a good thing.

Having said that, this is clearly a boy's thing. The spectators filling these slopes have the air of men who've got away from shopping, or visiting the mother-in-law, for a day. They're doing what Turkish blokes seem to enjoy doing, lighting fires in their portable braziers, grilling a few sausages, opening jerrycans of *raki* and smoking like chimneys.

I'm here with Yusuf Yavas, a local archaeologist. From the top of the hill we can see, in no particular order, a coach park, filling rapidly, a big bland estate of holiday homes and a canal built in the sixth century BC to connect Ephesus with the sea.

We're sitting on top of twenty-seven centuries of continuous human occupation.

'More Roman sites than Italy, more Greek sites than Greece' is how Yusuf describes this stretch of the Aegean coast, adding regretfully that his government doesn't attach a high priority to the work of himself and his colleagues.

He's fifty-two. His grandparents were originally Greek-speaking Muslims from Crete and Salonika who were forcibly moved out of their traditional homelands in the exchange of populations which followed fighting between Greece and Turkey after the First World War. Enormous hardships and ignominious loss of property were forced on two million people. Now he wants to see Turkey closer to the rest of Europe, away from the fanatics of right and left. I ask him why he thinks some Europeans are dragging their feet over Turkish admission. He puts it down to fears over religion and unemployment.

'Turkey is ninety-eight per cent Islamic country. Also unemployment rates in Turkey are quite high, I think European people think, OK, all the Turks will come to Europe and take our jobs.'

For a moment his mild manner slips.

'I think European people are not informed very well. They have an image in their heads of an Arabic country. Turkey is not Arabic. It's a secular country. We have democracy for about eighty years. They should learn more about Turkey.'

Then he smiles, a little apologetically.

'Maybe it's our fault too. We must express our feelings better.'

We're interrupted by a cheer from the crowd as the first camels are led into the arena below us. They're much bigger, taller and hairier than the camels I saw in the Sahara. They come from Iran where they breed two-humped with one-humped camels to produce this big single-humped breed. Not that one can see anything of the hump itself for it's obscured by the *hamut*, a sumptuously decorated wooden superstructure covered with silks and brocades, lengths of embroidered felt and carpet, a leather saddle and a bell which rings whenever they move. This edifice is both decorative and very heavy and causes the camel to sashay and sway like some great diva. Yusuf tells me that for the last three or four months they will have had to live from the fat stored in their humps as their trainers deliberately stop feeding them in order to increase their aggression. It's also their rutting season, so the combination of hunger and lust will, they hope, make for some good entertainment.

**Opposite**
*A simit-seller tempts the crowd with his bread rings coated in sesame seed.*

**Above left**
*Two heavyweight camels try to get each other's heads on the ground.*

**Above right**
*Contestants foam at the mouth. Not surprising as they're angry, hungry and randy.*

**Opposite**

*Selçuk. Camels gather beneath the arches of a Byzantine aqueduct. The elaborately decorated saddle (hamut) is put on four months before the wrestling, so they can get used to its weight.*

It may also explain why most of them, the camels not the trainers that is, are foaming at the mouth.

All the camels have names, and their pedigree is studied carefully by those who gamble on the outcome. Apparently a few years ago there was a fashion for calling camels Saddam, Bush and Clinton.

The atmosphere is, almost literally, intoxicating. Smoke, rich with the smell of tobacco and grilling meat, drifts across the hillside, along with the whining, thumping squeal of drum and pipe bands, whose relentless rhythm mingles with a P/A system booming out non-stop commentary from the podium.

Balloon- and candyfloss-sellers work the noisy crowd. The camel owners – men in suits with mobiles at their ears, well-dressed women inscrutable behind dark glasses – take their places in the VIP enclosure. The ring fills as the competing camels, some of whom may have spent eight to ten hours in a truck on the way here, get to stretch their legs, foam a bit and generally get angry. Each one is accompanied by a team of *urganci*, rope men, who follow their camel like dockers around a ship, ready to restrain their beast should things get out of hand.

As the tension rises the camels have their wicker muzzles removed, though their jaws remain restrained by thin string to prevent any serious biting. Then they're divided off into pairs. The unstoppable commentator's voice rises an octave and, finally, the wrestling begins.

Despite the foaming and the starvation and the randiness some of the camels seem remarkably uninterested in starting a scrap, and have to be raced towards their opponents by the *urganci*. Once they get locked together their necks seem to do most of the work, pushing against each other and occasionally entwining so that two heads appear to spring from one neck, a surreal parody of the double-headed Hapsburg eagle.

The camels are divided into three categories, roughly corresponding to small, medium and large, and after some inconclusive early bouts things move up a gear as the more popular heavyweights, roared on by their supporters, face up to each other.

One breaks away from its minders and gallops off across the ring, aiming straight for any other camel it can find. Two more collide so hard that one of them is completely lifted off its front legs and remains inelegantly suspended for quite some time as the other one tries to kick his back legs away. Which is not as easy as it looks, for the back legs, thin and spindly as they may appear, are, once splayed, as tough as steel cables.

There are certain established moves in camel-wrestling, which they call 'tricks'. Biting ankles and forelocks seems a speciality, and the headlock, with the opponent's head trapped between the two front legs, is much appreciated, except of course by the camel whose head it is. Ribbons of saliva fly everywhere as they push, grab, bite and lock before a winner is declared and the rope men rush in to haul the beasts apart.

In early afternoon, a near-perfect bout has the crowd on their feet. Two top-weight camels are, without doubt, wrestling. Leaning, twisting and grappling each other with their long, thickly maned necks. After a long stalemate, one begins to dominate, slowly forcing the neck of his opponent down onto the sand. Then the other flicks his neck away and they start again, until not only the head but the entire trunk of one of the camels flicks over and lies in the dust. What with the shrieks from the crowd, the manic thudding of drums, and the apoplectic ranting of the

commentator, I feel I've been knocked out too.

I've had a glimpse of another Turkey, away from metropolitan Istanbul. A glimpse of the strength of old traditions (the 20,000 crowd here was almost entirely Turkish). But even here there has been much change. Selçuk's population has doubled in the last twenty years and the once quiet bays of the Aegean are choked with holiday apartment blocks. But perhaps the most poignant image of change is the vehicle ahead of us as we leave the wrestling arena. It's a pick-up truck, and in the back, wrapped tight in a white canvas sheet, with only its head protruding, is a magnificent Iranian camel. For thousands of years his ancestors carried the trade that made Europe rich, Now he's another commodity.

## Day Forty-three: *Göreme, Cappadocia*

We're 300 miles east of Istanbul now, at a city called Kayseri. With a population of over a million, its thriving business parks and gleaming new automobile distribution centres are clear evidence that the commercial boom is not confined to Istanbul and the west. This is the heart of Anatolia, the ninety-five per cent of Turkey which is geographically part of Asia. Its size, both in land and population numbers, would, if accession were to go ahead, make Turkey by far the largest country in the European Union. And this worries a lot of Europeans.

Yet the history of this area links up with the very heart of European culture. In

**Above**

*Among the extraordinarily eroded pillars of volcanic rock in what they call The Valley of Love. I can't think why.*

the years after the birth of Christ, Kayseri, then called Caesarea, was where St Paul (born Saul in nearby Tarsus) began to make the first Christian conversions. The province of Cappadocia became the epicentre of the early Christian Church, and core beliefs such as the concept of the Holy Trinity were first formulated here by a group of leading ecclesiastical writers known as the Cappadocian Fathers.

Cappadocia was once a huge area, home to the Hatti and then the Hittites two to three thousand years before Christ. It was known as far back as the reign of King Darius of Persia as Katpatuka, the 'Land of Beautiful Horses'. Now the name refers only to a small area characterised by the weird and wonderful rock formations, some of which I am riding through, on a good-tempered grey called Bulu, in the company of Hasan Çalci, a local boy from Göreme who studied art and design in Italy and now runs one of the most beautiful of the cave hotels in Cappadocia.

All around us are tall thin pillars of honey-coloured rock which look like giant asparagus spears, or as most people seem to prefer, colossal phalluses. Indeed, so geologically aroused is the scenery that it's popularly known as The Valley of Love.

Millions of years ago a volcano, known to the ancient world as Mount Argaeus and now on my map as Erciyes Daği, erupted, spewing lava across a wide area. The compressed ash solidified into a soft rock called tufa, which was easily eroded by the wind and rain, but of such complex composition that the erosion was never uniform and rather than whole valleys being scooped out and washed away, vertical columns of rock have been left standing, like trees that have survived a forest fire.

Not all resemble giant phalluses; there are tall conical shapes, rectangular slabs and thin columns with precarious, table-like basalt caps, eroding much more slowly, perched on top. And behind the rock faces are elaborate troglodyte networks which often provided refuges for those fleeing religious persecution.

The most interesting of these is a complex near Göreme where thirty rock churches, out of an estimated thousand throughout Cappadocia, are clustered in a comparatively small area, now an open-air museum. These date back to anywhere between the sixth and eleventh centuries and one of them, the Dark Church, has an almost self-contained interior, with a set of mock architectural features, non-supporting columns and faux arched vaulting carved from the rock. The advantage of being the Dark Church, so called because this amazing place was lit by one small window, is that the rich and complex frescoes that cover the walls have been well preserved. The only damage to the robed figures and the biblical characters is that the eyes, and in some cases the mouths, have been scratched out. This is believed to have been done by Muslim Turks who took refuge in these caves after they'd been abandoned by the Christians, and who believed that the eyes carried some sort of curse.

**Above**
*With Andus Emge at one of the rock-carved Christian churches at the Göreme Open-Air Museum, many of which are over a thousand years old.*

Hasan's hotel in among the rocks is called the Anatolian Houses and every room is carved in a different shape and decorated with carefully chosen local artefacts. It's out of season at the moment and we have the place almost to ourselves. Hasan was born, the son of a carpet-weaver, in these caves he's converted. Starting out with just a donkey and an English dictionary, he began to show tourists around.

I ask him how much physical closeness to the Middle East (Syria is little more than 200 miles to the south) affects this part of Turkey.

'Of course we are believing in the same religion,' and here his brow furrows, 'but the mentality of our life is totally, totally different with Easterns than with Europeans. West has always been more exciting for the Turkish people.'


## Day Forty-four: *Göreme*

One of the best ways to see the spectacular Cappadocian landscape is from a balloon, and I'm all prepared to go up at first light this morning when the telephone by my bed rings and I'm given the bad news that our ascent has been cancelled owing to strong winds and the likelihood of snow.

Having sustained mild sunburn on the horseback ride yesterday, this comes as something of a shock, but when I peer out of the window there is no rosy-fingered dawn, but a leaden grey sky and a hissing wind that turn this eccentric landscape of rock stacks and fissured stone columns from friendly to vaguely sinister.

In Göreme the gift shops have their wares out, but few people are buying.

**Opposite**

*With Andus in his
hi-tech cave at the
Fairy Chimney Hotel,
Göreme.*

Walk up the hill to meet up with a German anthropologist and his wife who keep a guest house called The Fairy Chimney Hotel. It sounds a bit whimsical but there is a sound historical background to the idea of fairy chimneys. The Turks who rediscovered this area after much of it had been abandoned looked with some awe at the rock towers, many of which had small holes in the top where birds nested. They concluded, quite rightly, that no human beings could live up there, but, rather less rightly, that the inhabitants must therefore be fairies.

Andus Emge is a bit of a lone wolf amongst anthropologists. Trained at Heidelberg, his speciality was vernacular architecture, adobe mud dwellings, that sort of thing. He first came here as a student twenty years ago at a time when the Turkish government was encouraging those living in caves, fairy chimneys and the like, to resettle into newly built conventional houses. He returned in the 1990s, when the prevailing wisdom had begun to change. UNESCO had declared this both a World Heritage and Landscape Heritage area (leading, says Andus, to a double dose of bureaucratic confusion) and insisted that the old rock dwellings should be lived in after all, at the same time imposing restrictions on materials and design that put many people off.

In 1997 Andus paid the local council 25 euros rent a year and began work on a property that had been abandoned for so long that it was widely assumed to be haunted. He's done wonders, but there are aspects that would give any health and safety inspector minor heart failure.

Andus' workroom, for instance, is only accessible from a steep and narrow outside staircase with no rail of any kind to hold onto. A small hobbit-like door through which you have to bend double to enter gives onto a warm and womb-like room carved out of the rock. A cave it might be, but it's a cave with ADSL broadband access and the first I see of Andus, he's illuminated by the light from an Apple Mac screen.

Andus concedes that there were good reasons for resettling people. None of the rocks is altogether stable and there had been instances of people being killed by collapse. Degradation is inevitable, and he likens the chimneys to icebergs, slowly depleting all the time.

But the majority have been occupied quite safely for centuries, and his cave complex was once a monastery. They have all the usual advantages of being warm in winter and cool in the heat of summer and because the tufa is so soft, many of the usual home alterations can be done with a chisel or a pickaxe. If he wants a new shelf he just chisels an alcove out of the wall. And what's more, this is no below-ground cave. It's a chimney, a cave with a view. A troglodyte skyscraper.

Outside the rain has turned to snow and the buildings of Göreme, both natural and unnatural, have disappeared into a swirling white mist. We pick our way carefully down the now lethally slippery steps and into the living room, or more accurately, living cave, where Andus' Turkish wife Gülcan has prepared food and some tea.

Gülcan is a round-faced, merry lady some years younger than Andus, with braided black hair, a multi-bangled ethnic necklace, big attractive eyes and a mischievous smile.

When Andus came to live here, she remembers, he was considered to be either mad or possibly a secret agent. Her Turkish friends, especially the younger generation, were not interested in living in caves, seeing them as difficult to keep clean, impractical for all mod cons and quite possibly haunted. She herself is now

completed converted to life in a fairy chimney and refers to Andus as 'my good and lovely fairy', which embarrasses him. Rather happily.

After we've eaten, the talk turns to the strength of superstition round here and Gülcan invites me to meet a neighbour of theirs who can read fortunes from coffee grounds.

The three of us sit cross-legged on a divan whilst some strong Turkish coffee is prepared. After I've drained my cup the neighbour, a woman of early middle age with a sharp face framed by a headscarf, instructs me to put my saucer on top of my cup and turn the cup upside down. After allowing a few minutes for the residue to cool she asks me to lay a finger on top of the cup, make a wish, then turn cup and saucer the right way up and pass it over to her.

She studies the grounds on the saucer and on the side of the cup carefully, flicking her eye from one to the other.

While we're waiting, Gülcan talks up her neighbour's skills. She once told her mother that she would have a big fire in her house and, sure enough, two weeks later it happened. She also admits that, as far as the Islamic religion is concerned, reading coffee grounds is a sin.

'But I don't believe,' she says cheerfully.

'What if someone saw really bad news?' I ask her.

Gülcan's expression changes, and she casts a quick glance at the other woman.

'Once she told me she was reading for another neighbour and her brother was lost for some time and...' she lowers her voice to a whisper, 'she says I hope it will not happen, but I have seen a dead body in the coffee.'

However silly my rational self says these things are I can never have my fortune told without a slight drying of the mouth and dampening of the palms, so I'm relieved that there's nothing nasty to be seen. I will travel far. I must be careful of dark places where I will encounter snakes.

'Bad animals,' she confirms, but won't be drawn as to whether the snakes are pythons.

That is apparently the extent of the bad news. The good news provokes a lot of giggling between the two of them.

'You are going to meet with two different ladies. They are very beautiful and one is much richer than you.'

'Does the coffee indicate what my wife might think?'

'Ah,' says Gülcan, 'you have a wife too?'

I nod. More consultation.

'Well, there is a new love for you. In the Cappadocia area.'

They then break off for quite intense speculation around the coffee cup, broken by ever more frequent giggling. Gülcan nods significantly. 'Oh, that's interesting. You are going to meet this rich lady in the internet chat room.'

My impression is that the whole process has less to do with psychic penetration and more to do with a good old gossip. Coffee-reading is, Gülcan told me, very popular but eighty per cent of it is done by and for women. It's probably a good way of winkling out the scandal, talking about what they couldn't talk about just face to face. That's my theory.

Meanwhile I'm thinking of setting up a new website – Richladies.com.


**Day Forty-five:** *Göreme*

This morning's phone call brings good news. The wind has dropped, the skies are clear and conditions look ideal for our balloon flight. The only trouble is it's not yet six o'clock and it's pitch dark and bitterly cold. Not much talk as we're driven just outside the town to a clearing amongst the cones of rock, where two huge balloons are being prepared.

The pilot of my balloon is a Swede called Lars and his co-pilot is his English wife Kali. They have flown all over the world but are almost as excited about today's flight as we are. The air will be both clear and cool. Visibility should be near-perfect.

We're up in the sky about the same time as the sun, and for a while it is uncomfortably cold. The ride, though, is magnificent. The strange and unique landscape all begins to make sense as we rise above it. The eastern horizon is broken by the 12,848-foot peak of Erciyes Daği, its summit partly ripped away by the eruption that helped shape everything we can see. Long, flat tables of rock mark the height of the plateau created by the vast lake of lava, most of it now cracked, fissured and fashioned into the bluffs, cones and tall pillars that cover the ground like sentinels of some petrified army.

With the hard, bright sun at a low angle and a fresh-fallen blanket of snow on the ground, it's not only the rocks that stand out. We can see the fine detail of fields and orchards and vineyards. Though the volcanic rock makes for fertile soil, the climate has changed over the last few years and, according to Kali, the combination of warmer winters and late frosts has ruined harvests. Vines and apricot trees have

been worst affected and certainly the apricot orchards look especially vulnerable under the snow. Many farmers are turning to tourism instead, or leaving the area altogether.

'What used to be farms have now been abandoned,' she says, with the regret of someone who first fell in love with the area sixteen years ago. 'When everybody had a horse and cart and everybody worked the fields. Give it another ten years and I don't think we're going to recognise much.'

Lars seems less interested in what's happening on the ground than what's happening in the air. He reads the air currents with obsessive delight, alert to all the subtle shifts and patterns, such as the emptying of the cold air from the valleys as the land warms up. His greatest wish, he says, would be to be able to colour the air to show us the streams and eddies and waterfalls and rapids all around us, which only he seems to be able to see. He takes us up to 8,000 feet. From here the detail is less distinct. The rock forests of Cappadocia have given way to a wider view. From the Taurus Mountains in the south and to the rising Anatolian plateau to the east. Here the Tigris and Euphrates rivers, around which the earliest civilisations in the world were born, rise and run south to Iraq.

They sound very distant and very remote from our world, but if Turkey ever does join the European Union, and most of those I've talked to here want that to happen, then Europe will share its south-eastern border with Syria, Iraq and Iran. Now that would concentrate the mind.

**Above and overleaf**
*A cold clear morning in Cappadocia. Perfect conditions for ballooning and a perfect way to see this uniquely weird landscape, highlighted by a blanket of freshly fallen snow.*

113